Classic
MAIN COURSES

Classic
MAIN COURSES

Favourite traditional recipes
from the world's finest cuisines

APPLE

A QUINTET BOOK

Published by The Apple Press
6 Blundell Street
London N7 9BH

ISBN 1-85076-664-9

This book was designed and produced by
Quintet Publishing Limited
6 Blundell Street
London N7 9BH

Creative Director: Richard Dewing
Designer: Isobel Gillan
Project Editor: Anna Briffa
Editor: Patricia Burgess

Typeset in Great Britain by
Central Southern Typesetters, Eastbourne
Manufactured in Singapore by Bright Arts (Pte) Ltd
Printed in Singapore by Star Standard Industries (Pte) Ltd

The material in this publication previously appeared in:
*Cajun Cooking, Caribbean Cooking, Creole Cooking,
Nuevo Cubano Cooking, New Jewish Cooking, Lebanese Cooking,
Mexican Cooking, Greek Meze Cooking, The Fresh Pasta Cookbook,
Recipes from a Polish Kitchen, Portuguese Cooking, The Complete
Rice Cookbook, Russian Regional Recipes, Salsa Cooking,
Scandinavian Cooking, Southern Cooking, Spanish Cooking, Stir Fry
Cooking, Thai Cooking* and *Vietnamese Cooking*

CONTENTS

Introduction 7

Glossary 8

Poultry 15

Beef 47

Pork and Ham 71

Lamb 103

Seafood 127

Vegetarian 165

Index 190

INTRODUCTION

Drawing on a diversity of culinary traditions, *Classic Main Courses* presents a wealth of exciting ideas that will inspire adventurous cooks everywhere. Here you will find fragrant Thai curries, hearty Cajun stews, spicy Mexican hotpots, exotic Caribbean seafood, enticing Italian pasta, classic Russian roasts and rapid Oriental stir-fries – in fact, a taste of far-flung places without ever leaving your kitchen!

Perhaps you have always wondered how to make an authentic paella, or wanted to experiment with the unusual varieties of fish now available. Maybe you'd like to recreate some of the dishes you've eaten on foreign holidays. Or perhaps you simply want to inject some variety into your cooking repertoire. Whatever your reasons, this book has an abundance of ideas to call upon all of which guarantee to provide inspiration. The recipes are easy to follow and a comprehensive glossary of unusual ingredients is included. Everything required to make these international dishes can be bought in large supermarkets or ethnic grocers, but for those who may not have ready access to such outlets, local alternatives are suggested. So whether you live in London or Land's End, San Francisco or Smallville, the pleasures of foreign tables are never far away.

GLOSSARY

The international nature of this book means that some unusual ingredients are necessary for certain dishes. Many can be bought in large supermarkets, but others may be obtained from ethnic shops.

FRUIT

Plantain   A starchy member of the banana family, the plantain must be cooked. The flesh can be ivory, yellow or pink. It the recipe calls for green plantains, your task is straightforward: look for green-skinned plantains. These are starchy and not sweet. If ripe plantains are specified, look for ones that are turning from green to yellow-brown. If all you can find are green-skinned ones and your recipe calls for ripened, place them in an oven set at 150°C/300°F/Gas Mark 2 until the skin turns black and begins to split.

Calabaza   This large squash, the size of a football with orange flesh, is usually sold in wedges that look like pieces of pumpkin, although the texture and flavour of calabaza is somewhat sweeter. You can usually find this squash in West Indian grocers and market stalls. Hubbard or butternut squashes make good substitutes.

Breadfruit   A large round or oval green fruit used as a vegetable. It is best used when the skin is green rather than brown. The central core should be removed and the cream-coloured flesh eaten as a starchy vegetable, boiled, roasted or fried.

Chayote   Also called christophene, cho-cho, chu-chu and mirliton, this is a tropical squash-like fruit that resembles a green gnarled pear. It must be cooked and has a slightly citrus tang and a taste of cucumbers. Chayote keeps well, seldom losing its crunchy texture, and is available at many speciality shops and market stalls year-round.

Mirliton   See *Chayote.*

Ackee   Ackee is the fruit of an evergreen tree introduced into Jamaica from West Africa. It is reddish-yellow in colour, and when ripe it bursts open to display shiny black seeds covered by a creamy yellow flesh – this is the only edible section, and it has a soft texture resembling scrambled eggs. The fruit must *only* be eaten ripe – unripe *and* overripe ackee can be poisonous.

Tomatillos   Because of their appearance, tomatillos are sometimes called green tomatoes, or little tomatoes, and they are often (wrongly) used in place of tomatoes in salsa. In fact they are members of the Physalis family. They have a papery outer husk that must be removed, and they should be rinsed to get rid of the sticky residue on the surface of the husked tomatillo. Peek under the husk to see how ripe they are. Bright green tomatillos are not ripe; look for pale green to yellowish ones. If you use unripe tomatillos, the salsa will be tart. You can add a little sugar to offset the tartness.

Kaffir Lime   One of the most distinctive flavours of Thailand, this is a knobbly dark green fruit, of which only the aromatic zest and leaves are used in cooking – the juice makes a traditional hair shampoo. Use lime zest and citrus leaves as substitutes if you can't find the real thing, with dried kaffir lime to supplement the flavour.

VEGETABLES

Sweet Potato   A tuberous vegetable whose skin colour ranges from yellow to reddish-brown and pink. The flesh may be white, yellow or orange, and can be eaten boiled, baked, fried, or roasted. Ideal for both sweet and savoury dishes.

Jicama   A root vegetable, with an unusual flavour something between a raw potato or turnip, an apple, and a sweet radish. It should be peeled and eaten raw.

Galangal   A ginger-like rhizome, similar in appearance but milder in flavour. Sometimes also known as Siamese ginger. It is used in a similar way as ginger: fresh, dried or ground.

Vine Leaves   Vacuum-packed or tinned, and preserved in brine, vine leaves must be soaked and drained before use. They can be stuffed (*dolmades*) or used to wrap fish or game.

Banana Leaves   Are used for wrapping and cooking foods in; dark green, inedible and huge, they are often cut into smaller pieces for use.

Tofu   This white curd, normally about the consistency of a caramel custard, is made from unfermented soya bean paste. It is available in 'firm' and 'soft' forms, either plain or smoked.

Bean Curd   See *Tofu*.

Beansprouts   Sprouted mung beans, eaten raw or steamed, and used in stir-fries, soups and salads.

Bamboo Shoot   A long, fibrous shoot with a white central core. Usually bought canned, ready-peeled and par-boiled. They should be eaten as soon as possible after opening the can. They will, however, last for up to 6 days in a refrigerator if the water in which they are stored is changed daily. Only about 10 species of bamboo have shoots that are edible.

Wood Ear Fungus   Known under a variety of names. Perhaps the most common is derived from its habitat of decayed wood. The Chinese call it cloud ears because it resembles the clouds rendered with a paintbrush in a Chinese painting. It is also called Judas or Jew's ear from its botanical name (*Auricularia auriculajudae*).

It is valued for its subtle, delicate flavour and slightly crunchy 'bite'. It is always sold in its dried form and looks like a curly seaweed. When soaked, it expands to five times its dried size, so a little goes a long way. It should be rinsed thoroughly to wash out the grains of sand that seem to cling to it. It does not require long cooking and has no flavour of its own but readily absorbs seasonings. It does not like moisture and should be stored in a sealed container in a cool, dry place.

Lemon Grass (*citronella*)   This gives a lemony flavour to dishes, but is more aromatic than the lemon fruit. The lower several inches of the stalk are used, from the whitish 'bulb'. In soups and curries, the fibrous stalks are usually partly crushed by pounding with the back of a knife and removed before serving; another use is in some salads, in which case the stalks are cut into thin rings (it may be necessary to peel off the outer, more fibrous leaves). Available fresh, dried and ground.

CHILLIES

Chillies Exist in many varieties, varying in size and shape as well as colour and intensity of flavour. Generally, green chillies are milder than the red ones, and deseeding them reduces their intensity.

The chillies below are listed according to their strength, from the mildest to the hottest. However, it is difficult to give an exact guide, since the same type of chilli can vary widely in heat, depending on the growing conditions.

Anaheim Also known as the California chilli, this is pale green, 12–18 cm/5–7 in long, skinny and relatively flat. Mild in flavour, it is good roasted and peeled.

New Mexico This chilli resembles the Anaheim, although it is a little hotter. Green New Mexico chillies are available for only a short time each autumn outside New Mexico. Most are allowed to ripen to a bright red and are then dried. They are available in their dried form, and are the type used in *ristras*, hanging bunches of dried chillies.

Poblano These green-black chillies have broad shoulders, narrowing to the tip, and resemble dark, emaciated capsicum peppers. Moderately spicy, they are never eaten raw, but are roasted and peeled. Poblanos are often incorrectly called pasillas, both in their fresh and dried state.

Chipotle This is the jalapeño chilli, smoked and dried. It is hot, and adds a wonderful, smoky flavour to salsas and cooked dishes.

Jalapeño These glossy green chillies are probably most widely used variety outside Mexico. They are smooth-skinned, narrow and about 8 cm/3 in long. Although they are hot, their heat is much reduced if they are seeded and veined. They can be used raw, roasted, pickled, smoked, or dried. If left to ripen, they turn red.

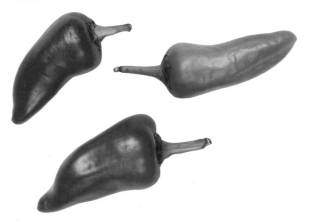

Serrano Slightly hotter than jalapeños, these are small, about 5 cm/2 in long and very skinny. They are ripe when dark green, but if left on the plant will continue ripening to a bright red. They are most often eaten raw in salsas.

Ancho This is the dried version of the poblano. It has a very pleasant spiciness that is hot but still easily tolerable. The ancho is often mislabelled pasilla, but is distinguishable when held up to the light by its red-brown colour; in the same light, a true pasilla is brown-black.

Habañero These chillies of the Yucatan, along with the related Scotch bonnet of the Caribbean, are just about the hottest chillies in creation. The habañero is not widely available fresh but is commonly used as an ingredient in bottled hot sauces. It looks like a miniature capsicum pepper or lantern, perhaps 5 cm/ 2 in long, and its colour can range from green to orange-red.

HERBS AND SPICES

Coriander Roots Used particularly in Thailand where they are ground together with the stems for curry pastes and sauces. The leaves are used in salads and as a garnish.

Filé Powder Ground sassafras leaf, which is used to season and thicken gumbo, a traditional Cajun fish stew. It can be hard to find outside Cajun country.

Allspice This flavouring is also known as pimento seed. It is the dark reddish-brown berry of a tree indigenous to Jamaica. After the berries are dried in the sun, they look like large peppercorns, but the scent and flavour are similar to a blend of cinnamon, cloves and nutmeg.

Star Anise The seed pods of one of the Magnolia trees. The tan-coloured, eight-pointed pods resemble stars, hence the name. When dried, a shiny, flat, light brown seed is revealed in each point. It has a pronounced liquorice flavour and the ground spice is one of the essential ingredients in the Chinese five-spice powder. In Vietnam it is used primarily in simmered dishes and for making stock.

Lebanese Spice Mix This does not have a standard name in Arabic, nor is there a standard recipe; it is devised by each cook to taste. It is made ahead of time, in order for the flavours to mingle, and used when required. A guideline proportion might be 4 parts ground cinnamon, 1 part ground cloves, 1 part ground chilli, 1 part green cardamom pods.

Annatto A rusty red dried seed from the tropical annatto tree. It is used to colour and flavour cooking oil.

Five-spice Powder An aromatic, Chinese spice powder, made according to an ancient formula using three native spices – star anise, cassia bark and Szechwan peppercorns – with the seeds of wild fennel and cloves from the nearby Moluccas or Spice Islands.

Garam Masala Literally 'hot mixture', this is a combination of spices, including chilli, black pepper and coriander seed, used as a flavouring in many Indian dishes.

SAUCES, PASTES AND FLAVOURINGS

Yellow Bean Sauce Made according to the ancient recipe for jiang or pickled yellow soya beans in a salty liquid. It is normally bought in cans and jars but it is best transferred to a jar in which it can be stored in a refrigerator almost indefinitely.

Chilli Sauce A condiment or paste made from chillies, salt, sugar and vinegar, available in bottles in various strengths.

Fish Sauce An essential ingredient in Thai cooking and as a condiment. Salty and fermented, it is highly distinctive, a clear brown liquid sold in bottles. Use either the Thai version, Nam Plaa, or the Vietnamese Nuoc Mam; they are virtually identical. In cooking, use straight from the bottle; for using as a condiment, serve in small Chinese sauce dishes with 2 or 3 chopped small chillies and a squeeze of lime juice. Fish sauce is rich in salt and some nitrogen; Thais sprinkle a few drops, taken with a spoon, on dishes in much the same way that salt and pepper are used at a Western table.

Shrimp Paste A pinkish or dark brown paste used for flavouring Thai dishes. It is available in the West in vacuum-sealed jars.

Tahini A paste made from ground, toasted sesame seeds emulsified with olive oil, lemon juice and garlic. This basic staple of Lebanese and Arabic cuisine can be made at home, but is often bought prepared in bottles (preferable to the tinned variety). It is used to make dips and other dishes, but can also be used on its own as a dip.

Palm Sugar This thick, brown, almost wet sugar is made from the boiled sap of the Palmyra palm tree. It is usually available canned in the West.

Arak A spirit distilled from grape juice and flavoured with aniseed. Similar to Greek ouzo, it is somewhat lighter in flavour and less syrupy in consistency.

Hoisin Sauce The barbecue sauce of Southeast Asia. Made from red rice, which is coloured with a natural food dye, usually annatto seeds, it is a sweet-tasting, thick, reddish-brown sauce best used as a condiment for roast pork and poultry.

It is made from fermented soya bean paste, sugar, garlic and spices, normally five-spice.

Nuoc Mam *(fish sauce)* A powerfully flavoured pungent seasoning sauce. It is very much an acquired taste, and substitutes such as soy sauce are often sufficiently exotic to Western palates.

MEAT

Weijska   These Polish smoked sausage rings are available from large supermarkets or good delicatessens. It is a chunky ham and pork sausage which is well flavoured with garlic. Delicious served boiled and sliced with cabbage or sauerkraut.

Andouille Sausage   This is a spicy Cajun smoked-pork sausage. Some gourmet delicatessens sell it, otherwise your best bet is to go for Polish kielbasa – but since Andouille supplies part of the spicy flavour in some recipes, be sure to adjust the seasonings if you use something else.

Kabanos   This long, thin smoked Polish cooked sausage is readily available from supermarkets and delicatessens. Delicious with sauerkraut or cabbage.

Chorizo   Chorizo is a spicy Spanish sausage, most often made with pork but sometimes with beef. Paprika is usually the predominant spice, but the ingredients may vary widely, and the seasonings in a dish containing chorizo should be adjusted accordingly. The fat content also varies. Chorizo adds excellent flavour to beans and eggs.

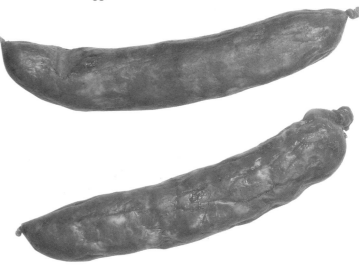

Oyster Sauce   One of the most popular bottled sauces in Southeast Asia. Made from dried oysters, it is thick and richly flavoured. Many people use it as a superior version of soy sauce, but Asians use it as an accompaniment for stir-fried vegetables and to flavour and colour braised and stir-fried dishes.

Tabasco Sauce   The brand name of a Louisiana hot sauce made on Avery Island, deep in Cajun country. Very hot red peppers are ground with salt, fermented in oak barrels, then pickled with vinegar. Other manufacturers make similar hot-pepper sauces.

Hot Pepper Sauce   See *Tabasco*.

Soy sauce   Made from fermented soya beans mixed with a roasted grain, normally wheat. It is injected with a yeast mould and after fermentation begins, salt is added. Yeast is added for further fermentation and the liquid is left in vats for several months and then filtered.

Light soy sauce is thin, salty and light in flavour and is used as a condiment and in cooking where its light colour will not spoil the colours of the ingredients, particularly seafood.

Dark soy sauce is thicker with a full-bodied flavour and is used to add colour where needed. Generally, it is less salty than the light soy sauce. The Chinese mushroom soy sauce is made with the addition of flavourings from Chinese straw mushrooms.

Morcela   A Spanish type of black pudding used in meat and vegetable dishes. If unavailable, morcilla can be used instead.

Tasso   A very highly seasoned smoked pork or ham, Tasso is rarely used as the star ingredient, but as a flavouring in jambalayas and other dishes. You may substitute another type of smoked ham, but add more cayenne and other seasonings if you want the dish to be spicy.

FISH

Pompano   A gourmet fish, delicious and very expensive. It lives in the Atlantic Ocean and the Caribbean. It is moderately fatty and firm textured, and does not fry well. It is excellent stuffed with crab and baked whole, or grilled. Substitute whole rainbow trout or flounder fillets.

Flying Fish   An unusual silver-blue winged fish with a white, slightly salt flesh and a large number of bones. It is found off the coasts of Barbados.

Salt Cod   Originally taken to the Caribbean as food for slaves by the Colonists. Of all the salted fish, cod seems to have the best flavour. To remove the salt, wash well and soak for several hours or overnight in cold water.

Red Snapper   Similar to sea bass, red snapper has a lean but firm flesh with a distinctive flavour. If not available, substitute any white, firm-fleshed fish, such as perch, turbot or sole.

Carp   A freshwater fish, having a 'muddy' flavour and the larger fish are very coarse. However, if you order carp from the fishmonger you will buy a farmed fish. The fish must not be too small or large and it must be perfectly fresh. Ask the fishmonger to scale the fish as the scales are large and they do get everywhere, even if you are careful about holding the fish down in the sink under running water. The cooking smell is not altogether pleasant but the poached flesh is moist, white and has a delicate flavour. It cannot be compared directly with white sea fish such as cod or haddock, which are drier, more distinctive in flavour and with flesh that flakes; it is better to compare it with a large salmon trout for texture. Carp has lots of very large, fine bones.

NOODLES

Rice noodles are available in three sizes: wide and flat, spaghetti-sized and very thin vermicelli-sized, also known as rice stick noodles. Sometimes sold fresh, they are usually dried and either deep-fried or soaked before using.

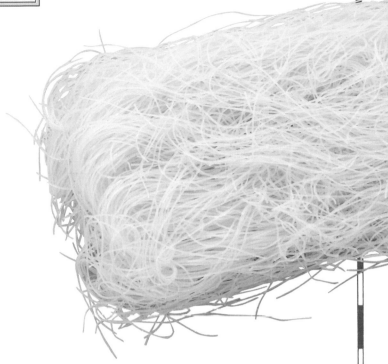

Cellophane or glass noodles (also known as bean-thread or transparent noodles) are semi-clear and made from the dried, strained liquid of puréed mung beans; sold dried, they need to be soaked for 15 minutes before cooking.

Egg noodles are made from egg and wheat flour, and are sold fresh and dried, often in compressed parcels. They vary in size.

GRAINS AND PASTRY

Buckwheat   Available from healthfood shops, buckwheat is usually sold roasted. The grains are small and slightly angular in shape. Although it is thought of as a cereal, buckwheat is not a true cereal in botanical terms. It is cooked in about 1½ to 2 times its volume of water by bringing it to the boil, then leaving the grain to absorb the liquid. Butter is forked into the buckwheat, which is then known as kasha. Kasha is a popular accompaniment for meats and stews; it is also used to stuff cabbage leaves.

Hominy   This is maize treated with lye; it tastes surprisingly different from untreated maize. It comes in various forms, including the old Southern 'hominy grits', and canned. One of its main uses is in posole (see page 82).

Filo   A pastry made from flour, water and oil originally developed in ancient Greece. It is rolled extremely fine, almost paper thin, and is used for both sweet and savoury pastries. Filo is available from supermarkets.

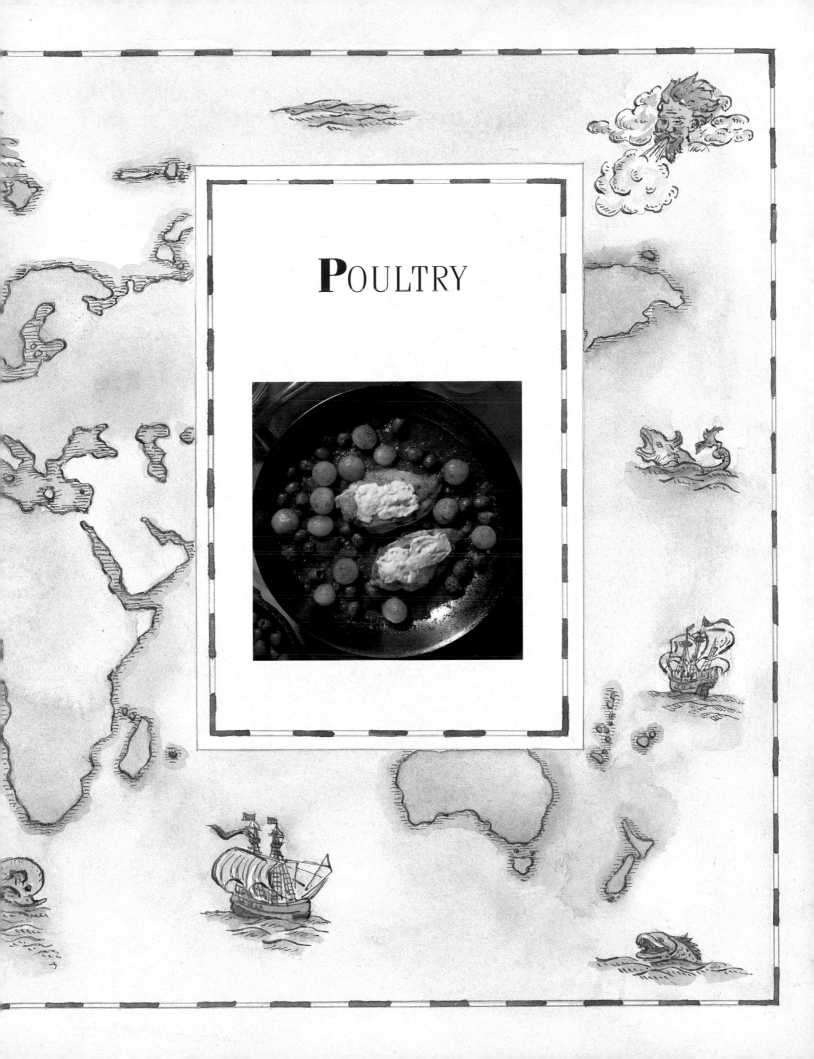

POULTRY

CHICKEN CILANTRO

— MEXICO —

This is an elegantly simple dish. It is rather rich, so it is ideal as part of a long-drawn-out meal, where each course is fairly small. A large serving might be overwhelming!

SERVES 4–6

1 small onion
at least 1 garlic clove
4 tbsp olive oil or butter
   (or a mixture of the two)

4 small chicken breasts,
   skinned and boned
salt and pepper
225 g/8 oz fresh
   coriander leaves

■ Chop the onion and garlic, and fry them together in the olive oil and/or butter until the onion is, in the Spanish term, 'crystalline' (tender and transparent).
■ Cut the chicken into 2.5-cm/1-in cubes. Fry with the onion and garlic until the chicken is cooked through: this should take no more than 5 to 10 minutes, depending on the temperature and the size of the cubed chicken. The meat should be browned slightly on the outside, but only in places. Add the chopped coriander leaves and seasoning; stir for a few seconds to coat. Serve with plain boiled rice and the pan juices.
■ For a much stronger-flavoured (and darker-coloured) sauce, deglaze the pan with half a glass of dry white wine or vermouth.

STUFFED CHICKEN

— LEBANON —

Stuffed poultry is a favourite all over the Arab world, from Morocco – where stuffing is made with couscous, cinnamon and pickled lemon pieces – to Lebanon and Syria, where the staple ingredient varies between burghul and rice, both of which are usually enriched with nuts and herbs.

SERVES 6

50 g/2 oz butter
225 g/8 oz minced lamb
1 large onion, finely
   chopped
2 tbsp pine nuts
1 tbsp raisins
225 g/8 oz long-grain
   rice

salt and freshly ground
   black pepper
600 ml/1 pt water
1 tbsp honey
3 tbsp Greek-style yoghurt
2-kg/4½-lb free-range
   roasting chicken

■ Heat 1 tablespoon butter in a frying pan. Gently sauté the lamb, stirring to ensure it browns all over. Transfer the meat with a slotted spoon to a plate, add another 1 tablespoon butter to the pan and stir in the finely chopped onion. Sauté over medium-low heat for about 5 minutes, until it is limp; add the pine nuts and continue to sauté until both onions and nuts are lightly coloured. Add the raisins and rice, and stir for a minute or two until the rice is transparent: season to taste. Pour in the water and bring to the boil. Reduce the heat, cover and simmer for about 25 minutes, or until the rice has absorbed all the water. Leave to cool.
■ Preheat the oven to 200°C/400°F/Gas Mark 6. Melt the remaining butter in a saucepan, take off the heat; stir in the honey until it melts, then the yoghurt. Stuff the chicken with the rice mixture, and secure the opening with skewers. Leave the remaining rice in the pan to be warmed up later. Place the chicken in a roasting pan and baste with the yoghurt sauce.
■ Roast for 20 minutes at the above temperature, then reduce the heat to 180°C/350°F/Gas Mark 4 for a further 1¼ to 1½ hours. Baste twice with the yoghurt sauce. Test to see if the chicken is cooked by piercing the joint between body and thigh with a skewer; the juice should run clear.
■ Heat the remaining rice gently over low heat and moisten with a little of the chicken pan juices. Serve with the hot stuffed chicken.

HONEY-RUM CHICKEN WITH MUSHROOM SAUCE

PUERTO RICO

*This is a classic Creole recipe. Serve the sauce over the chicken
and accompany with cooked vegetables, pasta or rice.*

SERVES 4

4 large chicken breasts,
    boned, skinned and fat
    cut off
50 ml/2 fl oz orange juice
1 tbsp honey
20 g/¾ oz clarified butter
2 garlic cloves, crushed
125 g/4 oz button
    mushrooms, sliced
125 g/4 oz oyster
    mushrooms, sliced

225 ml/8 fl oz dark rum
450 ml/¾ pt chicken stock
salt and freshly ground
    black pepper
125 ml/4 fl oz single
    cream
2 eggs, beaten
2 tbsp chopped fresh
    coriander
orange slices, to garnish
    (optional)

■ Poke several holes in the chicken breasts with a knife
point. Mix the orange juice and honey and marinate
the chicken in it for 20 minutes. In a large heavy-based
frying pan, brown the chicken in 15 g/½ oz clarified
butter. Remove from the heat and set aside.

■ Melt the remaining butter in the same frying pan,
then add the garlic and mushrooms and fry for 1
minute. Pour in the rum and flame it. Add the chicken
stock, salt and pepper and chicken and simmer over a
low heat for 30 minutes. Just before serving, beat the
cream with the eggs and add to the frying pan. Cook
over low heat for about 1 minute. Add the coriander,
check the seasoning and cook for a further 1 minute.
Garnish with orange slices, if desired, and serve.

LEMON CHICKEN

GREECE

*Chicken flavoured with lemon is a delicious combination of tastes
and one that is commonly found in Greece. There is plenty
of sauce in this dish, so rice would be a welcome accompaniment.*

SERVES 6–8

50 g/2 oz butter
1.6-kg/3½-lb prepared
   chicken, without giblets,
   cut into small portions
salt and freshly ground
   black pepper, to taste
300 ml/½ pt boiling water
1 bunch spring onions,
   trimmed and cut into
   2.5-cm/1-in pieces

3 eggs
3 tbsp freshly squeezed
   lemon juice
2 tbsp chopped fresh dill,
   to garnish

■ Melt the butter in a large, heavy-based saucepan and
add the chicken. Cook for about 5 minutes, or until
evenly browned, turning and rearranging during
cooking.

■ Season the chicken with salt and freshly ground
black pepper and add the boiling water and spring
onions. Cover and simmer for 35 to 40 minutes, or until
the chicken is tender and cooked through.

■ Place the eggs in a small bowl and beat well.
Gradually whisk in the lemon juice, a little at a time, to
prevent curdling. Whisk in 300 ml/½ pt of the cooking
liquid from the chicken. Pour the egg and lemon
mixture over the chicken and stir continuously until the
sauce has thickened slightly. Do not boil.

■ Transfer the chicken and sauce to a warm serving
dish and sprinkle with the chopped fresh dill.

CHICKEN WITH WALNUTS AND POMEGRANATES

IRAN

Pomegranates are one of the most symbolic fruits in Jewish history. They are significant for Rosh Hashana *(the New Year). This braised chicken with walnuts and pomegranates is one of the most prized dishes among Iranian Jews. Serve with rice.*

SERVES 4

1 roasting chicken, 1.6–
   1.8 kg/3½–4 lb
salt
freshly ground black
   pepper
2 tbsp vegetable oil
1 onion, finely chopped
275 g/9 oz walnuts,
   ground or finely
   chopped
450 ml/¾ pt pomegranate
   juice, or 125 ml/4 fl oz

syrup diluted with
   375 ml/12 fl oz water
2 tbsp lemon juice
75 ml/2½ fl oz boiling
   water
1 tbsp tomato purée
2 cinnamon sticks
2 tbsp light brown sugar
watercress, pomegranate
   seeds and walnut halves
   for garnish

■ Rinse chicken under cold running water and dry inside and out with kitchen paper. Season skin and cavity with salt and pepper.

■ In a large casserole over medium-high heat, heat oil. Add chicken and cook until golden brown, turning frequently to allow all sides to brown, 10 to 15 minutes. Remove to a large plate and set aside.

■ Into pan, stir onion. Cook until soft, 2 to 3 minutes. Stir in ground or chopped walnuts and cook until well browned, 2 to 3 minutes. Pour in pomegranate juice or syrup mixture, lemon juice and boiling water. Stir in tomato purée, cinnamon sticks and brown sugar and bring just to a boil. Reduce heat to low.

■ Return chicken to pan and cook, covered, until chicken is tender and juices run clear when leg is pierced with a knife or skewer, 45 to 50 minutes. Remove chicken to a serving platter and cover with foil to keep warm. If sauce is too thin, bring sauce up to a boil and reduce until thickened slightly.

■ Pour sauce over chicken, garnish platter with watercress and pomegranate seeds and arrange walnut halves over top.

RED CHICKEN CURRY

THAILAND

SERVES 6

1.25 ltr/2 pt thin coconut
   milk
2 tbsp chilli paste
10 white peppercorns,
   crushed
325 g/11 oz chicken
   breasts, boned, skinned
   and cut across into
   5-mm/¼-in thick slices
3 tbsp fish sauce

½ tbsp palm sugar
7 small white aubergines,
   quartered
3 fresh red chillies,
   quartered lengthwise
2 kaffir lime leaves, torn
   into small pieces
20 g/¾ oz sweet basil
   leaves

■ Heat 225 ml/8 fl oz of the coconut milk in a pan, stir in the chilli paste and white peppercorns, and cook for 2 minutes. Add the chicken slices, mix well and add the rest of the coconut milk. Bring to a boil, then add the fish sauce and palm sugar. Boil for 1 minute and then add the aubergine, chilli and lime leaf. Bring back to the boil, cook for 3 minutes, add the basil, remove from the heat and serve.

POACHED CHICKEN WITH MELON

—— CUBA ——

SERVES **4**

375 ml/12 fl oz chicken
  stock
4 chicken breasts, skinned,
  boned and trimmed of
  fat
3 tbsp red wine vinegar
1 tbsp firmly packed dark
  brown sugar
2 garlic cloves, crushed
1 tsp finely chopped fresh
  root ginger

1 tsp Dijon mustard
50 g/2 oz orange-flesh
  melon balls
50 g/2 oz yellow-flesh
  melon balls
75 g/3 oz diced mango
freshly snipped chives to
  garnish (optional)

■ In a medium-sized frying pan, bring stock to a boil, then reduce heat to low and simmer. Add chicken, cover and simmer until cooked through and the juices run clear, 8 to 10 minutes. With slotted spatula, remove chicken from pan. Leave to cool, then cover and refrigerate until chilled, about 2 hours.

■ Meanwhile, boil stock until reduced to 125 ml/ 4 fl oz. Stir in remaining ingredients, except melon and mango, and cook, stirring frequently, 5 minutes. Gently stir in melon balls and diced mango. Toss to coat. Refrigerate until chilled, 2 hours. Garnish with snipped chives and serve.

CHICKEN ANDOUILLE AND PRAWN JAMBALAYA

—— UNITED STATES ——

All the spiciness in this jambalaya comes from the meat. Be sure to taste before you serve, and adjust seasonings, especially if you've had to substitute other ham or sausage for the Tasso and Andouille.

SERVES **6 – 8**

1 tsp salt
½ tsp cayenne pepper
½ tsp black pepper
1½ tsp fresh or ½ tsp dried
  thyme
1 uncooked chicken
  breast, skinned and
  cubed
2 tbsp vegetable oil
3 celery stalks, chopped
2 onions, chopped
2 green peppers, chopped
2 garlic cloves, finely
  chopped
125 g/4 oz Tasso or other
  smoked ham, chopped

175 g/6 oz Andouille or
  other spicy sausage,
  sliced
450 g/1 lb tomatoes,
  seeded and chopped
225-g/8-oz tin tomato
  sauce
225 ml/8 fl oz poultry or
  seafood stock
225 g/8 oz medium
  prawns, shelled and
  deveined
125 g/4 oz spring onions,
  chopped
575 g/1¼ lb cooked rice,
  to serve

■ In a small bowl, mix together the salt, cayenne, black pepper and thyme. Toss the chicken in it, until well coated with spices.

■ In a large frying pan or Dutch oven, heat the oil. Sauté the chicken, stirring almost constantly, until the chicken is browned, 6 to 8 minutes. Add the celery, onion, green pepper and garlic, and sauté until the vegetables are limp, about 5 minutes.

■ Stir in the ham, sausage, tomatoes, tomato sauce and stock, and cook until mixture is bubbling. Reduce the heat and simmer until tomatoes have cooked down and liquid is slightly reduced, creating a rich, red broth. Add the prawns and cook until they are opaque and tightly curled, 2 to 3 minutes. Taste and adjust the seasonings. It should be very spicy. Add the spring onions and enough rice so that the mixture is neither soupy nor dry.

CHICKEN IN BLUE

ITALY

Blue cheese makes a rich sauce for chicken or turkey. Serve large quantities
of plain fresh pasta noodles to balance the full flavour of the sauce.
I have used Danish blue but any other blue cheese may be substituted –
dolcelatte, for example, or tangy Gorgonzola for a really powerful flavour.

SERVES **4**

2 tbsp olive oil
1 garlic clove, crushed
1 red pepper, seeded and
diced
450 g/1 lb boneless
chicken, skinned and
diced
salt and freshly ground
black pepper
225 g/8 oz small button
mushrooms

4 tbsp dry white wine
150 ml/¼ pt single cream
225 g/8 oz Danish blue
cheese, cut into small
pieces
2 spring onions, finely
chopped
2 tbsp chopped parsley

■ Heat the oil in a large frying pan. Add the garlic, red pepper and chicken with some seasoning – go easy on the salt at this stage as the blue cheese can make the sauce quite salty. Cook, stirring often, for about 20 minutes, or until the diced chicken is lightly browned and cooked.

■ Add the mushrooms and cook for 2 minutes, then pour in the wine and bring to the boil. Turn the heat to the lowest setting and make sure the mixture has stopped boiling before pouring in the cream and stirring in the cheese. Stir over low heat until the cheese has melted. Do not allow the sauce to simmer or it will curdle.

■ When the cheese has melted, taste the sauce, then pour it over the pasta and sprinkle with spring onions and parsley. Serve at once.

CHICKEN SALAD WITH GRAPEFRUIT, MINT AND LEMON GRASS

VIETNAM

SERVES 6

vegetable oil for deep frying
about 40 prawn crackers, purchased
1 tbsp unsalted peanuts
1 tbsp sesame seeds
25 g/1 oz dried prawns, soaked in hot water for 30 minutes
50 g/2 oz pork belly
50 g/2 oz uncooked prawns in the shell
salt
1 medium cucumber, unpeeled, halved lengthways, seeded and sliced thinly
1 large carrot, shredded
50 g/2 oz fresh beansprouts
25 g/1 oz cooked chicken meat, cut into thin strips
1 tbsp chopped mint
½ tbsp chopped lemon grass
1 large grapefruit, peeled, sectioned and cut crossways into 2.5-cm/1-in pieces
coriander sprigs, to garnish

EGG PANCAKES
2 eggs
¼ tsp Nuoc Mam sauce
freshly ground black pepper
vegetable oil

DRESSING
1 garlic clove, crushed
1 fresh red chilli pepper, seeded and crushed
½ tbsp sugar
½ tbsp fresh lime juice
½ tbsp rice vinegar

■ Heat about 5 cm/2 in oil to 180°C/350°F in a wok. Add the chips two or three at a time and keep them immersed in the oil with a pair of chopsticks or slotted spoon until puffy. This should take about 10 seconds. Turn and cook for the same length of time. When finished, set aside.

■ Rub down the wok, return it to a moderate heat and cook the peanuts. Stir constantly until the peanuts are golden brown – about 5 minutes. Grind with a grinder or put between a couple of sheets of clean, strong paper and crush with a rolling pin or milk bottle. Toast the sesame seeds in the same way for only 3 minutes. Grind lightly to a grainy texture.

■ To make the pancakes, beat the eggs, Nuoc Mam sauce and pepper together with ½ teaspoon water in a bowl. Brush the bottom of a non-stick omelette pan with some oil and place over moderate heat until hot. Pour in half the egg mixture and tilt the pan immediately to spread it evenly over the bottom – the pancake should be paper-thin. Cook until the egg is set – this should not take more than 30 seconds. Turn and cook on the other side for about 15 seconds. Set aside. Repeat, using up the rest of the mixture and set aside.

■ Combine the garlic, chilli, sugar, lime juice, vinegar and Nuoc Mam sauce in a bowl. Stir to blend thoroughly. Set the dressing aside.

■ Drain the dried prawns and pound or blend in a blender or processor until very fine. Set aside.

■ Cover the pork with water and bring to the boil over a high heat. Lower and boil for about 30 minutes or until the juices run clear when the meat is pierced with a knife. Run cold water over the pork and set aside.

■ Cook the raw prawns in boiling water until just pink – about 2 minutes. Run cold water over them, drain, peel, devein and cut lengthways in halves. Shred the prawns and set aside.

■ Sprinkle salt over the cucumber and carrot and leave to stand for 15 minutes. Run cold water over them and squeeze dry with your hands. It is imperative that the vegetables are bone dry to ensure their crunchiness.

■ Dip the beansprouts in salted boiling water for 30 seconds. Run cold water over them and drain.

■ Cut the egg pancakes into strips. Combine the strips with the dried prawns, shredded prawns, chicken, cucumber, carrot, beansprouts, mint, lemon grass, grapefruit and sesame seeds. Mix well with your hands, then pour in the dressing.

■ Transfer to a serving dish or serve individually, and sprinkle the ground peanuts over it. Garnish with coriander. Serve with prawn crackers on which guests place bite-sized portions of the salad. Alternatively, serve in hollowed grapefruit shells instead of one large serving dish.

SALSA CHICKEN

MEXICO

SERVES 4

25 g/1 oz plain flour
1 tsp ground cumin
1 tsp paprika
½ tsp salt
¼ tsp pepper
4 chicken breasts, boned and halved
1–2 tbsp vegetable oil
about 6 tbsp chicken stock (optional)

SALSA

450 g/1 lb tomatoes, seeded and chopped
2 garlic cloves, crushed
75 g/3 oz onion, finely chopped
4 jalapeño chillies, chopped, with some seeds included
1 tbsp. cider vinegar

■ To make the salsa, in a medium saucepan, simmer the tomatoes, garlic and onion for 10 to 15 minutes, uncovered, to evaporate excess liquid from the tomatoes. Add the jalapeños, vinegar and oregano, and simmer for 5 minutes more. Add salt to taste.

■ Mix the flour with the cumin, paprika, salt and pepper. Sprinkle it over the chicken breasts and turn the chicken so all sides are coated with the mixture. Heat the oil in a large frying pan. Add the chicken pieces and brown them on both sides, then stir in 175 g/6 oz of the salsa. (The remainder will keep well if frozen and may be used as a dip with corn chips.) If the salsa is very thick, add the chicken stock. Simmer the chicken until cooked through, 20 to 30 minutes, occasionally spooning the salsa over the top. Serve over rice or noodles.

EASTER CHICKEN CASSEROLE

DENMARK

SERVES 4–6

50 g/2 oz butter
1.5 kg/3 lb chicken joints
3 medium onions, chopped
600 ml/1 pt chicken stock
225 g/8 oz mushrooms
2 tbsp chopped fresh parsley

salt and pepper
225 g/8 oz peas
2 eggs, size 4 or 5
2 tbsp milk
butter for cooking
2 tbsp cornflour

■ Melt the butter and fry the chicken joints and onions until golden brown. Add the chicken stock, mushrooms and 1 tbsp of the chopped parsley and season with salt and pepper. Cover and simmer for 35 minutes, adding the peas for the last 5 to 8 minutes.

■ Beat the eggs and milk together and season. Fry the egg mixture in a little butter in an omelette pan until firm. Put the chicken and vegetables on a heated serving dish and keep warm. Thicken the cooking liquid with the cornflour blended with water to make the gravy. Pour the gravy over the chicken and vegetables. Cut the fried egg into thin strips and use to garnish the chicken with the remaining parsley.

CITRUS-FRIED CHICKEN

UNITED STATES

SERVES 4

50 ml/2 fl oz fresh lime
  juice
50 ml/2 fl oz fresh lemon
  juice
50 ml/2 fl oz fresh orange
  juice
50 ml/2 fl oz olive oil
4 garlic cloves, peeled
  and crushed

few drops Tabasco sauce
1 chicken, jointed
125 g/4 oz flour
1 tsp salt
½ tsp black pepper
vegetable oil or lard

■ Make the marinade by mixing fruit juices, olive oil, garlic and Tabasco. Trim any excess fat off the chicken and remove skin, if desired. Put the chicken pieces in a glass or other non-reactive dish. Pour the marinade over the chicken, making sure that each piece is coated. Marinate in refrigerator at least 3 hours, or overnight.

■ Mix flour, salt and pepper in a bowl or a paper bag. Dip or shake each chicken piece in the flour mixture so that there is a thin coating of flour over the entire piece. Shake off any excess.

■ Heat oil or lard in a heavy frying pan. The oil should be about 1–2.5 cm/½–1 in deep and very hot. Carefully place chicken in the hot oil. The pieces should not be crowded. You will probably need to fry the chicken in two batches (keep the first batch warm in the oven while the second is cooking), or use two frying pans. Fry over medium to medium-high heat, depending on your stove and the heaviness of the frying pan. Watch carefully so that the chicken does not burn. It is done when the meat juices run clear, about 20 to 25 minutes.

CHICKEN BROCHETTES WITH ORANGE SAUCE

FRANCE

SERVES 4

700 g/1½ lb chicken
  breasts
rind and juice of 2
  oranges
1 tbsp oil
salt and freshly ground
  pepper

SAUCE
4 tbsp redcurrant jelly
25 g/1 oz butter
4 tbsp red wine
2 cloves
¼ tsp ground nutmeg
juice of 2 oranges
4 tbsp water
1 tsp cornflour

GREEN RICE RING
225 g/8 oz cooked long-
  grain rice
3 tbsp chopped parsley
1 spring onion, finely
  chopped
salt and freshly ground
  pepper
3 tbsp salad oil
1 tbsp white wine vinegar

GARNISH
orange slices

■ Skin and trim the chicken breasts. Remove bone if it is still attached. Cut into 2.5-cm/1-in pieces. Mix half the orange rind with all the orange juice, oil and seasoning and pour over the chicken pieces. Allow to stand in the refrigerator for at least 1 hour. Turn over from time to time to allow juice to penetrate. Thread the chicken pieces on to skewers.

■ To make the sauce place all the ingredients, except the water and cornflour, in a saucepan with the remainder of the marinade. Allow to simmer gently for 10 minutes.

■ Preheat the oven to 180°C/350°F/Gas Mark 4. To make the rice ring mix the cooked rice with the parsley, spring onion and seasoning. Mix the salad oil and vinegar separately and pour over the rice. Pack into a well-oiled ring mould. Heat in the oven for 15 minutes.

■ Brush the chicken brochettes with oil and cook under the grill, turning from time to time for about 10 minutes: 2 minutes under a high heat each side and the remaining time under a medium heat.

■ Finish the sauce by blending the cornflour with the water. Add some heated sauce to the cornflour mixture and return to the saucepan. Stir until the mixture thickens slightly.

■ Turn out the rice ring on to a heated serving plate and place the brochettes on top. Garnish with slices of orange. Serve the sauce separately.

CARIBBEAN COCONUT CHICKEN

BARBADOS

SERVES 4

4 chicken breasts, halved, boned, skinned and fat cut off
2 tbsp vegetable oil
1 large red sweet pepper, cored, seeded and diced
1 large green sweet pepper, cored, seeded and diced
1 large onion, chopped
1 garlic clove, crushed
50 g/2 oz unsweetened coconut flakes, toasted
2 tsp grated lime rind
salt
25 g/1 oz butter or margarine
¼ tsp sweet paprika
¼ tsp hot pepper sauce
1 tbsp lime juice
1 tbsp apricot preserve
fresh coriander, to garnish (optional)

■ Preheat the oven to 180°C/350°F/Gas Mark 4. Pound the chicken to 8mm/¼ in thickness between two sheets of cling film and set aside. Heat the oil to medium hot in a large frying pan and fry the peppers, onion and garlic for about 10 minutes, stirring frequently, until slightly soft. Remove from the heat. In the same pan, stir in the coconut, lime rind and salt to taste.

■ Spoon one-eighth of vegetable mixture over the centre of each chicken breast. Bring the long ends of each breast up over the filling and secure with cocktail sticks. Place the butter or margarine in a small roasting tin and melt over medium heat. Place the chicken rolls, seam-side down, in the tin. In a small bowl, combine the paprika, hot pepper sauce and ½ teaspoon salt and sprinkle the mixture over the chicken rolls. Bake for 25 to 30 minutes until the chicken is cooked through and juices run clear when the roll is pierced with a knife. Remove the rolls to a chopping board.

■ Stir the lime juice and apricot preserve into the drippings in the roasting tin and bring to the boil, stirring to loosen browned bits on the bottom of the tin and to blend. Remove from the heat.

■ Remove the cocktail sticks from the chicken rolls and cut into 1 cm/½ in slices. Arrange the slices on a serving dish and pour the sauce over. Garnish with fresh coriander, if desired.

SWEET AND SOUR CHICKEN

THAILAND

A dish that is popular with most people. It is not spicy but a spoonful of fish sauce will add zest.

SERVES 4–6

900 ml/1½ pt peanut or corn oil
425 g/15 oz chicken breasts, boned, skinned and cut across into 5-mm/¼-in slices
plain flour for coating
1 medium-sized onion, sliced
1 medium-sized green pepper, sliced
125 ml/4 fl oz tomato ketchup
125 g/4 oz tomato quarters
50 g/2 oz diced pineapple
125 ml/4 fl oz chicken stock
2 tsp soy sauce
1 tsp sugar
1 tsp white vinegar

■ Heat the oil in a wok or frying pan, coat the chicken lightly with flour and fry it until light brown, about 5 minutes. Remove and drain on kitchen paper. Remove all the oil, except for about 75 ml/3 fl oz. Add the onion and pepper, cook for 1 minute, mix in the ketchup, and then add the remaining ingredients. Stir-fry for 1 minute, add the chicken and continue to cook until the onion is tender, about 2 minutes. Serve with rice.

MUSTARD-BAKED CHICKEN

UNITED STATES

Coated with a sauce of mustard and soured cream, this Cajun dish is easy and tasty. Americans like to use cornbread to mop up the juices on their plates.

SERVES 6-8

125 ml/4 fl oz soured cream
50 ml/2 fl oz whole-seed mustard
175 g/6 oz cornbread, finely crumbled (see below)
1½ tsp fresh thyme or ½ tsp dried
1 tsp salt
¼ tsp black pepper
¼ tsp cayenne pepper
2 chickens, about 1.25–1.5 kg/2½–3 lb each, cut into serving pieces

60 g/2½ oz butter, melted

CORNBREAD
40 g/1½ oz plain flour
175 g/6 oz cornmeal
¾ tsp salt
1 tsp sugar
1 tbsp baking powder
2 eggs, lightly beaten
225 ml/8 fl oz milk
50 ml/2 fl oz melted butter

■ First make the cornbread. Set the oven at 200°C/400°F/Gas Mark 6. Lightly butter a 20-cm/8-in square baking pan.

■ In a medium bowl, combine all the dry ingredients. In a small bowl, mix together the eggs, milk and butter. Pour these into the flour mixture and stir by hand, making sure there are no lumps.

■ Pour into the prepared tin and bake until a knife inserted into the cornbread comes out clean, 18 to 22 minutes. Cut into 9 squares.

■ In a small bowl, combine the soured cream and mustard. In another small bowl, mix together the cornbread crumbs and seasonings. Spread the mustard mixture over the chicken pieces, then roll the chicken in the crumb mixture. Arrange the chicken in a single layer in large, shallow baking dish and drizzle with the melted butter. Bake at 190°C/375°F/Gas Mark 5 until the chicken is golden brown and the juices run clear if tested with the tip of a knife, about 1 hour.

MUSCAT BAKED ALMOND CHICKEN

LEBANON

Both a wine-making and a dessert grape, the muscat gives a pungent flavour to this recipe, which has its roots in a centuries-old tradition of using ground almonds as a thickening agent.

SERVES 6

2-kg/4½-lb chicken
salt and freshly ground pepper
½ tsp cinnamon
large pinch nutmeg
fresh lemon thyme
fresh marjoram
225 g/8 oz muscat grapes, skinned, seeded and halved

225 ml/8 fl oz sweet muscat wine
1 tbsp butter
3 tbsp sliced, blanched almonds
50 g/2 oz ground almonds
150 ml/¼ pint single cream
2 egg yolks

■ Wash and pat dry the chicken, rub it all over with salt and pepper to taste, then the cinnamon and the nutmeg. Take 2–3 sprigs of lemon thyme and the same of marjoram and put them inside the chicken. Place it in a casserole, stuff with half the grapes and pour over the wine. Cover and cook the chicken in a preheated oven, 200°C/400°F/Gas Mark 6, for 1½ hours.

■ Remove the chicken from the oven and transfer it to a warm serving platter. Remove the grapes and herbs from the cavity, joint the chicken and cover it with foil to keep it warm.

■ In a small saucepan, melt the butter and sauté the sliced almonds for a few minutes until just coloured. Remove with a slotted spoon and set aside. Skim the fat from the chicken cooking juices in the casserole and strain them into the saucepan. Heat the juices gently until very hot, but not boiling, and stir in the remaining grapes and the ground almonds. Allow to cook for a few minutes to combine.

■ In a small bowl beat the cream and egg yolks together lightly. Take a spoonful of the hot chicken stock and stir it into the egg. Remove the saucepan from the heat and stir in the egg mixture to thicken.

■ Pour some of the sauce over the jointed chicken and sprinkle it with the toasted almonds. Pour the remainder into a sauceboat to serve with pilau rice.

Sautéed Chicken Compote

— BARBADOS —

SERVES 4

4 large chicken breasts, boned, skinned and cut in 1-cm/½-in strips
50 g/2 oz curry powder
50 g/2 oz clarified butter
1 ripe papaya, peeled, seeded (seeds reserved) and cut into 2-cm/¾-in chunks

2 bananas, cut crossways into 8-mm/¼-in slices
25 g/1 oz unsweetened coconut flakes, toasted
125 ml/4 fl oz dark rum
75 g/3 oz coconut cream
½ tsp salt
½ tsp white pepper

■ Dredge the chicken strips in curry powder. Melt the clarified butter in a large frying pan over high heat. Stir in the chicken and sauté until golden brown. Add the papaya, bananas and coconut flakes. Add the rum, which will ignite, and let the alcohol burn off.

■ Add the cream of coconut and simmer until heated, then season with salt and pepper. Stir quickly and serve immediately with a chilled green salad topped with your favourite vinaigrette and sprinkled with papaya seeds.

Chicken with Pounded Almond Sauce

— SPAIN —

The Arabs conquered Spain right up to the Pyrenees, and this dish is a reminder of their influence. The sauce is thickened with spiced, crushed nuts.

SERVES 4

2 garlic cloves, finely chopped
2–4 tbsp olive oil
1 thick slice bread
salt and freshly ground black pepper
1.25-kg/2¾-lb corn-fed chicken, in pieces
125 ml/4 fl oz chicken stock
10 strands saffron, soaked in a little stock

125 ml/4 fl oz fino sherry or Montilla
1 bay leaf, crumbled
25 toasted almonds
1 tbsp parsley, chopped almost to a paste
pinch of ground ginger
pinch of ground clove
1 tsp lemon juice

■ Fry the garlic quickly in 2 tablespoons of oil in a wide, shallow casserole. Remove to a blender or mortar. Over a high heat fry the bread quickly in the oil on both sides, then reserve.

■ Season the chicken pieces and fry them till golden on all sides (a corn-fed chicken should not need more oil). Remove from the pot and drain off any fat. Add the stock, saffron and fino, stirring to deglaze the bottom. Return the chicken pieces and add the bay leaf. Cook gently, covered, for 10 minutes.

■ Grind the toasted almonds in the blender or mortar with the garlic already there, adding the bread in pieces, the chopped parsley and remaining spices. Stir this aromatic purée into the chicken juices, with the lemon juice, and serve.

COCHIN-STYLE CHILLI CHICKEN

— INDIA —

SERVES 4

2 tbsp lemon juice
1 tsp salt
2 tbsp sugar
2 tbsp vegetable oil
10–12 fresh or dried curry leaves, or 1 tsp curry powder
350 g/12 oz shallots, sliced
6 garlic cloves, finely chopped
2.5-cm/1-in piece fresh root ginger, finely chopped
5 medium-hot green chillies, seeded and very finely sliced

2 medium tomatoes, chopped
½ tsp turmeric
¼ tsp chilli powder
1 chicken, 1.5–1.6 kg/ 3–3½ lb, jointed into 8 pieces
225 ml/8 fl oz water
2 tbsp fresh coriander, chopped
fresh coriander leaves and lemon wedges for garnish

■ In a small bowl, place lemon juice, ¼ teaspoon salt and sugar; stir to dissolve. Set aside.

■ In a casserole or large, deep frying pan, heat oil over medium-high heat. Add curry leaves or curry powder and stir until they sizzle, 10 to 15 seconds. Stir in shallots, garlic, ginger and chillies and cook until the shallots have softened and begin to colour, 5 to 7 minutes. Stir in tomatoes, turmeric, chilli powder and remaining salt. Cook 3 to 4 minutes longer.

■ Add chicken to vegetable mixture, moving pieces around to cover with some vegetables. Stir in the water and bring just to a boil. Reduce heat to low and cook, covered tightly, 20 minutes, stirring once.

■ Uncover and stir in reserved lemon-juice mixture and chopped coriander. Increase heat to medium and cook, uncovered, until sauce is slightly reduced, basting chicken occasionally, about 10 minutes.

■ Arrange chicken pieces on a serving platter. Pour sauce over and garnish with coriander leaves and lemon wedges.

CHICKEN AND CHICK-PEA STEW

RUSSIA

The Russians have a spicy condiment sold as Aintab Red Pepper here in the West. Since it is difficult to find, two thin, medium-hot red peppers have been substituted here.

SERVES 6

4 strands saffron
90 ml/3½ fl oz hot water
10 garlic cloves, crushed
2 fresh, thin, medium-hot
  red peppers, seeded
  and chopped
4 tbsp vegetable or
  sunflower oil
salt and freshly ground
  black pepper
1.5 kg/3 lb chicken
  breasts and thighs,
  washed and dried

2 tbsp ground coriander
1 tsp dried oregano
2 x 400-g/14-oz cans
  plum tomatoes, drained
450 ml/¾ pt water
575-g/1¼-lb can chick-
  peas, drained
2 tbsp lemon juice

■ Soak the saffron in hot water for 10 minutes. Place the saffron and liquid, garlic and peppers in a blender or food processor. Process until finely chopped.

■ Heat the oil in a casserole over medium-hot heat. Season the chicken to taste and sauté in batches until lightly browned. Remove to a plate and keep warm.

■ Reduce the heat and add the garlic purée. Stir with a wooden spoon for 2 minutes, than add the ground coriander and oregano. Stir for a further 2 minutes, then add the tomatoes. Break them up with the spoon while cooking for 3 minutes, then add the water. Add the chicken pieces and spoon the sauce over them. Bring to the boil, cover, and simmer for 20 minutes.

■ Add the chick-peas and continue to cook, covered, for a further 15 minutes. Remove the lid, stir in the lemon juice and increase the heat. Boil for 5 minutes to reduce the sauce. Serve immediately.

ROAST CHICKEN WITH BUCKWHEAT

POLAND

*If you would prefer to stuff the chicken with a breadcrumb mixture,
try the dill stuffing described at the end of the recipe.*

SERVES 4–6

175 g/6 oz roasted
  buckwheat
475 ml/16 fl oz water
1 onion, finely chopped
25 g/1 oz butter
1 garlic clove, crushed
125 g/4 oz chicken livers,
  chopped

½ tsp dried marjoram
salt and freshly ground
  black pepper
1 egg, beaten
1.5-kg/3-lb oven-ready
  chicken

■ Place the buckwheat in a sieve and rinse under cold running water. Put the buckwheat in a saucepan and pour in the water. Heat very gently until the water is just about simmering. Remove the pan from the heat, cover and leave for 30 minutes, by which time the buckwheat should have absorbed all the water.

■ Cook the onion in the butter for 10 minutes, until soft but not browned. Add the garlic and chicken livers and cook for a further 5 minutes, stirring occasionally, until the pieces of liver are firm. Add this mixture to the buckwheat with the marjoram and seasoning to taste. Stir in the egg to bind, making sure all the ingredients are thoroughly combined.

■ Preheat the oven to 180°C/350°F/Gas Mark 4. Rinse the chicken under cold running water, drain well and pat dry with kitchen paper. Spoon the stuffing into the body cavity and truss the bird neatly, tying string around the legs and wings. Place in a roasting tin. Roast for 1¾ hours, or until the chicken is golden, crisp and cooked through. Halfway through cooking, pour a little water into the bottom of the roasting tin and keep topping this up as it evaporates.

■ Transfer the cooked chicken to a warmed serving plate. Add a little extra water to the cooking juices, if necessary, and boil the liquid, scraping all the roasting residue off the pan. When the gravy is reduced and flavoursome, check the seasoning and serve.

VARIATION

To make a dill stuffing, cook 1 small onion in 25 g/1 oz butter until soft. Mix the onion with 175 g/6 oz fresh white breadcrumbs, 4 tablespoons chopped fresh dill, salt and freshly ground black pepper and 2 egg yolks. Whisk the whites until they peak softly, then stir into the stuffing.

CHICKEN WITH FETA AND GREEN OLIVES

—— GREECE ——

This dish originates from a small village called Barthouna, near Sparta. It is prepared with either olives or raisins, both being major products of this region.

SERVES 4

4 chicken breasts
flour, for dredging
salt and freshly ground
    black pepper
6 tbsp olive oil
350 g/12 oz button
    onions (or use large
    onions, quartered)
400-g/14-oz can chopped
    tomatoes

125 ml/4 fl oz boiling
    water
300 g/10 oz pitted green
    olives, washed and
    drained
1 tbsp red wine vinegar
125 g/4 oz feta cheese,
    sliced thinly

■ Arrange the chicken breasts on a chopping board, dredge with the flour and season with salt and freshly ground black pepper on both sides.

■ Heat the oil in a large, deep frying pan and add the chicken breasts, skin-side down. Cook on both sides for 3 to 5 minutes or until browned. Lift the chicken breasts out of the pan and set aside.

■ Add the onions to the frying pan and sauté for about 5 minutes or until softened, stirring frequently. Return the chicken to the pan and add the chopped tomatoes and boiling water. Season with salt and freshly ground black pepper, cover, and simmer for 25 to 30 minutes or until the chicken is tender and cooked through, adding a little extra boiling water if necessary.

■ In the last 10 minutes of cooking time, add the olives and vinegar. Stir to combine. Place a slice of feta cheese on top of each piece of chicken and continue to cook, uncovered, for a further 10 minutes, or until the cheese has just melted. Serve immediately.

CALYPSO CHICKEN

JAMAICA

SERVES 6

1.5-kg/3-lb chicken, cut
into 5-cm/2-in pieces
½ lemon
2 tsp salt
freshly ground black
pepper
2 garlic cloves, crushed
1 tbsp vinegar
¼ tsp chopped fresh thyme
25 g/1 oz butter or
margarine

2 tsp brown sugar
oil for frying
125 g/4 oz cashew nuts
125 g/4 oz mushrooms,
sliced
3 onions, chopped
6 slices fresh root ginger
50 ml/2 fl oz water
1 tbsp plain flour

■ Wash the chicken in cold running water, rubbing with the lemon. Season with the salt, pepper, half the crushed garlic, the vinegar and thyme. Leave to marinate for 3 hours.

■ In a large saucepan, melt the butter or margarine, then add the sugar. When it is bubbling, add the chicken and brown the pieces.

■ Meanwhile, in a frying pan, heat some oil. Fry half the cashews, then set them aside. In the same pan, fry together the remaining crushed garlic, the mushrooms, the other half of the cashews, onions and ginger. Add the water and pour the mixture into the large saucepan over the chicken. Cook for 25 minutes or until the chicken is cooked.

■ Mix the flour with some warm water and stir into the chicken mixture to thicken. Cook for 3 more minutes, then sprinkle with the remaining fried cashews. Serve with boiled rice.

CHICKEN AND HAM LASAGNE

ITALY

This is easy and delicious! Turkey may be used instead of chicken
– a great way of using up the Christmas roast.
Add any leftover stuffing to the sauce too.

SERVES 6-8

350 g/12 oz fresh
  lasagne verdi
2 quantities béchamel
  sauce (see below)
225 g/8 oz skinned,
  boneless cooked
  chicken, diced
225 g/8 oz lean cooked
  ham, diced
125 g/4 oz button
  mushrooms, chopped
6 spring onions, chopped
2 tbsp chopped parsley
1 tbsp chopped sage
salt and freshly ground
  black pepper
75 g/3 oz Caerphilly,
  Lancashire or
  Wensleydale cheese,
  finely crumbled

paprika
25 g/1 oz fresh white
  breadcrumbs

BÉCHAMEL SAUCE
1 thick onion slice
1 bay leaf
1 mace blade
2 parsley sprigs
600 ml/1 pt milk
40 g/1½ oz butter
40 g/1½ oz plain flour
salt and freshly ground
  white or black pepper

■ Lower the pieces of pasta one at a time into a large saucepan of boiling salted water. Bring back to the boil and cook for 3 minutes. Drain and rinse under cold water. Lay the pasta on absorbent kitchen paper. Butter a 30 38 x 20 cm/12–15 x 8 in ovenproof dish and set the oven at 180°C/350°F/Gas Mark 4.

■ Now make the béchamel sauce. Place the onion, bay leaf, mace and parsley in a saucepan. Add the milk and heat slowly until just boiling. Remove from the heat, cover and leave for 45 minutes.

■ Strain the milk into a jug or basin. Wash the saucepan, then melt the butter and stir in the flour. Slowly pour in the milk, stirring all the time. Continue stirring until the sauce boils, then reduce the heat, if necessary, so that it just simmers. Cook for 3 minutes, stirring occasionally. Add seasoning to taste.

■ Set aside one third of the béchamel sauce, covering it with dampened greaseproof paper to prevent a skin forming. Mix the chicken, ham, mushrooms, spring onions, parsley and sage with the rest of the sauce. Taste for seasoning, then layer this sauce in the dish with the lasagne, ending with a layer of lasagne on top. Stir the cheese into the reserved sauce (it doesn't matter if the sauce is too cool for it to melt), then spread it over the top of the pasta. Sprinkle with a little paprika and top with the breadcrumbs.

■ Bake for 40 to 50 minutes, until the topping is crisp and golden and the lasagne layers are bubbling hot.

CHICKEN WON TONS WITH VEGETABLES

CHINA

SERVES 4

4 chicken breasts, skinned
and boned
¼ tsp five-spice powder
8 spring onions, chopped
1 tsp sesame oil
5 tbsp soy sauce
1 garlic clove, crushed
1 egg, beaten
3 tbsp oil
2 celery sticks, cut into fine
2.5-cm/1-in strips
1 red pepper, quartered,
seeded and cut into thin
strips

½ medium head Chinese
cabbage, shredded
3 tbsp dry sherry

WON TON DOUGH
175 g/6 oz plain flour
50 g/2 oz cornflour
pinch of salt
1 egg, beaten
125 ml/4 fl oz water

■ First make the won ton dough. Sift the flour, cornflour and salt into a bowl, then make a well in the middle. Add the egg and pour in the water. Use a spoon to mix the egg and water into the flour. When the mixture binds together, scrape the spoon clean and use your hand to work the dough into a small ball, leaving the bowl free of mixture.

■ Place the dough on a clean surface and knead it thoroughly until it is very smooth. Cut the dough in half, wrap each portion in cling film, then set aside for 15 to 30 minutes.

■ Cut the chicken into 50 small pieces. Place them in a basin and add the five-spice powder, 2 tablespoons of the spring onions, sesame oil, 2 tablespoons of the soy sauce and the garlic. Mix well, cover and leave to marinate for 30 minutes.

■ Dust a work surface with cornflour and roll out one portion of dough into a 38-cm/15-in square. Cut the dough into five 8-cm/3-in strips, then across into squares. Brush a square of dough with beaten egg. Place a piece of chicken in the middle of it, then fold the dough around the chicken and pinch it together well. Continue filling the squares, placing them on a platter dusted with cornflour as they are ready. Roll out the second portion of dough and make a further 25 won tons.

■ Grease a large covered dish with oil and set it to warm. Bring a large saucepan of water to a boil, then cook the won tons in batches, allowing 5 minutes after the water has come back to a boil. Drain, transfer to the dish and keep hot.

■ Heat the oil in a large frying pan. Add the celery and pepper and stir-fry for 5 minutes. Add the remaining spring onions and cook for a further 2 minutes. Then add the Chinese cabbage and cook for 3–5 minutes. Pour in the remaining soy sauce and sherry and stir for 1 minute. Serve at once with the won tons.

CHICKEN PILAF

GREECE

*The classic Greek way to finish preparing this dish, and also
many others which use pasta or rice, is to brown some butter
in a small pan and pour it over just before serving.*

SERVES 6–8

125 g/4 oz butter
900 g/2 lb chicken
 breasts, skinned, boned
 and cut into bite-sized
 pieces
salt and freshly ground
 black pepper
pinch of ground cinnamon
pinch of ground allspice

2 onions, chopped
3 tbsp tomato purée
600 ml/1 pt boiling water
225 g/8 oz long grain
 rice
50 g/2 oz butter
chopped fresh mint, to
 garnish

■ Melt the butter in a large, heavy-based saucepan and sauté the chicken pieces for 5 to 10 minutes or until lightly browned, turning during cooking. Add salt, pepper, cinnamon and allspice, and stir well.

■ Add the onions to the saucepan and continue to cook until softened. Stir in the tomato purée and boiling water. Cover and cook for 20 minutes; then add the rice. Cover and continue to simmer for a further 20 to 25 minutes or until the chicken is cooked through and the rice is tender.

■ Remove the cover for the final 10 minutes of the cooking time to allow the liquid to be absorbed. Melt the butter in a small frying pan and cook until browned. Turn the pilaf out on to a warm serving platter and pour the browned butter over the top. Sprinkle with chopped fresh mint to serve.

CHICKEN BAKED WITH POTATOES AND GARLIC

PORTUGAL

SERVES 6

1.5-kg/3-lb chicken, cut into 12–16 pieces
1 kg/2¼ lb yellow waxy potatoes, quartered
1 onion, sliced
20 small–medium sprigs of rosemary
salt and pepper
8 tbsp olive oil
20 garlic cloves, unpeeled

■ Preheat the oven to 220°C/425°F/Gas Mark 7.
■ Put the chicken, potatoes, onion, rosemary and seasoning into a large, shallow baking dish. Mix together and then pour over the oil. Scatter the garlic cloves over the top and bake for 20 minutes.
■ Lower the oven temperature to 190°C/375°F/Gas Mark 5 and bake for about 45 minutes, turning the chicken and potatoes occasionally, until the chicken is cooked, the potatoes golden and the garlic crisp.

CHICKEN POT PIE WITH CORNMEAL CRUST

UNITED STATES

This version of old-fashioned chicken pot pie is made with a comforting mixture of chicken and mushrooms as its main ingredients. If you prefer, you can substitute peas and carrots for part of the mushrooms. Some people also like to add a little diced ham to the filling.

SERVES 6

60 g/2½ oz butter
1 small onion, chopped
350 g/12 oz mushrooms, sliced
4 tbsp flour
375 ml/12 fl oz chicken stock
125 ml/4 fl oz double cream
1 tsp salt
¼ tsp pepper
pinch of cayenne pepper
450–575 g/1–1¼ lb cooked chicken, cubed

CRUST
125 g/4 oz flour
150 g/5 oz cornmeal
1 tbsp sugar
1 tbsp baking powder
1 tsp salt
1 egg, lightly beaten with fork
225 ml/8 fl oz milk
4 tbsp melted butter

■ Sauté the onion and mushrooms in 45 g/1½ oz of the butter for 6 to 8 minutes, until the mushrooms are very tender. In a small saucepan heat but do not brown the remaining butter, then add the flour. Cook over low heat, stirring constantly, until the roux is a tan colour. While the roux is cooking, bring the chicken stock to the boil. When the roux is done, add a little of the stock to the roux, then gradually stir in the rest. Add the cream, the mushrooms, seasonings and the chicken. Mix well. Pour into a deep 25-cm/10-in pie dish.
■ To make the crust, preheat oven to 200°C/425°F/Gas Mark 7. Mix the flour, cornmeal, sugar, baking powder and salt in a medium bowl. In a small bowl, combine the egg, milk and melted butter. Pour the liquid ingredients into the dry ingredients and stir until the flour is evenly moistened. Spoon the mixture over the top of the chicken filling. Bake until the crust is golden brown, about 40 minutes.

CHICKEN AND **R**ICE **S**TEW

PUERTO RICO

SERVES 6

1 garlic clove, chopped
½ tsp dried oregano
½ tsp salt
1.5-kg/3-lb chicken, cut into 8 pieces
50 g/2 oz butter or margarine
1 small onion, finely chopped
75 g/3 oz green peppers, chopped
4 ripe tomatoes, skinned and chopped

350 g/12 oz uncooked long-grain white rice
1.75 ltr/3 pt chicken stock
freshly ground black pepper
300 g/10 oz frozen peas
50 g/2 oz Parmesan cheese, freshly grated
1 fresh hot pepper, chopped

■ Mix the garlic, oregano and salt together in a large bowl. Add the chicken pieces and mix them well together. Heat the butter or margarine in a saucepan and brown the chicken pieces. Transfer them to a plate.

■ Add the onion and green peppers to the pan and cook until soft. Add the tomatoes and browned chicken pieces, coating them well with the onion, peppers and tomato mixture. Reduce the heat and simmer for 30 minutes or until the chicken is cooked.

■ Transfer the chicken to a plate and leave to cool a little. Remove the bones and cut the flesh into 5-cm/2-in pieces.

■ Meanwhile, add the rice, stock and freshly ground black pepper to the tomato mixture and bring to the boil. Reduce the heat, cover and simmer for 20 minutes or until the rice is cooked. Stir in the peas, Parmesan and hot pepper. Mix well, then add the chicken. Cover and simmer for 2 more minutes, then serve.

ROAST GOOSE WITH FRUITY STUFFING

ISRAEL

SERVES 6–8

3.6–4.5-kg/8–10-lb young
   goose, thawed if frozen
salt
freshly ground black
   pepper
1 tbsp vegetable oil
1 large onion, chopped
6–8 tart apples, peeled,
   cored and cut up
75 g/3 oz raisins
200 g/7 oz prunes,
   chopped
100 g/3½ oz dried
   apricots, chopped
400-g/14-oz can cooked,
   peeled chestnuts
½ tsp dried sage, crumbled
1 tbsp chopped parsley
1 tbsp arrowroot
125 ml/4 fl oz apple juice
1 tbsp cider vinegar
watercress and apple
   slices for garnish

■ Remove all excess fat from inside and outside goose. Cut off fatty skin flap near tail. Rub skin and sprinkle cavity with salt and pepper. Prick skin all over.

■ In a large frying pan, over medium-high heat, heat vegetable oil. Add onion and cook until softened, 4 to 5 minutes. Add apples, raisins, prunes, apricots and chestnuts, and sprinkle with sage and parsley. Stir in 2 tablespoons water and cook just until liquid evaporates, 2 to 3 minutes. Remove from heat and cool slightly.

■ Preheat oven to 230°C/450°F/Gas Mark 8. Spoon stuffing into goose cavity and close with skewers or sew with kitchen string. Place goose on its back in a roasting tin and roast 30 minutes. Reduce oven to 180°C/350°F/Gas Mark 4. Remove goose from oven, pour off any fat and prick goose all over again. Turn goose on to its breast and roast for 1½ hours longer, removing fat from the tin and basting 3 or 4 times. When no more fat is being released, add 250 ml/8 fl oz water to roasting tin and continue roasting until goose is done. Remove to a serving platter, cover with foil and leave to rest 20 minutes in a warm place.

■ Pour off all but 1 tablespoon fat from the tin drippings. Stir arrowroot, apple juice and vinegar together and add to tin with 125 ml/4 fl oz water, adding more water if necessary. Season with salt and pepper to taste. Bring to a boil, stirring and scraping up any bits from the tin. Reduce heat and simmer 5 minutes. Strain into a gravy boat. Arrange watercress and sliced apples around the goose and serve gravy separately.

TURKEY ESCALOPES WITH WHITE WINE AND MUSHROOM SAUCE

FRANCE

SERVES 4

2 large turkey breasts,
   boned
1 tbsp flour
¼ tsp paprika
25 g/1 oz butter
2 tbsp vegetable oil
1 medium-sized onion,
   peeled
125 g/4 oz mushrooms,
   washed and sliced
2–3 tbsp white wine

SAUCE
300 ml/½ pt milk
1 slice of onion
1 bouquet garni
1 bay leaf
4 peppercorns, slightly
   crushed
20 g/¾ oz butter
3 tbsp flour
salt and white pepper

■ Cut the turkey breasts in half, place the halves between sheets of foil or cling film and beat out to an escalope shape with a rolling pin. Mix the flour with the paprika and coat the turkey.

■ Heat the butter and oil in a frying pan and over medium to high heat fry the escalopes on both sides until golden. They will need about 5 minutes each side. Keep warm in a low oven.

■ Cut one thick slice from the onion and cut the remainder into fine dice. Over a low heat cook the onion in the pan with oil from the turkey. After 3 minutes add the mushrooms and stir occasionally. Add the wine and leave for 2 minutes over a very low heat.

■ Meanwhile, put the milk with the slice of onion, bouquet garni, bay leaf and peppercorns on a low heat. Allow to come to almost boiling point. Then turn the heat off. Leave to infuse for 10 minutes covered.

■ Melt the butter in a small saucepan, add the flour and make a roux. Stir for 1 minute, then strain in the infused milk gradually to make a béchamel sauce. Cook until smooth. Add the onion and mushroom mixture and cook for a further 2 to 3 minutes. Serve on a bed of plain boiled rice.

GRILLED SPICY-MARMALADE TURKEY CUTLETS

—————— JAMAICA ——————

Canned pineapple slices may be used in this recipe, but if you're using fresh pineapple, save the crown and use it as a garnish. This dish can be done on the barbecue or a conventional grill.

SERVES 4

6–8 pineapple rings or 1 medium pineapple, cut lengthways into quarters with rind on and then scored crossways into 2.5-cm/1-in thick slices
1 orange, cut into 1-cm/½-in thick slices
20 g/¾ oz demerara sugar
225 g/8 oz marmalade
2 tbsp finely chopped spring onion

½ tsp crushed garlic
½ tsp hot pepper sauce
¼ tsp grated root ginger
½ tbsp Worcestershire sauce
½ tbsp vegetable oil
salt and freshly ground black pepper
4 turkey cutlets, about 1 cm/½ in thick

■ About 1 hour before serving, prepare the outdoor grill for barbecuing. Sprinkle the pineapple and orange slices with brown sugar.

■ In a small bowl, mix the marmalade, spring onion, garlic, hot pepper sauce, root ginger, Worcestershire sauce, oil and salt and pepper.

■ Arrange the turkey cutlets and fruit on the grill over medium heat. Cook for 5 to 7 minutes, brushing the turkey frequently with marmalade-spice mixture, and turning the turkey and fruit occasionally, until the turkey just loses its pink colour throughout.

■ Alternatively, preheat the grill. Prepare the marmalade mixture as above and arrange the fruit, with the pineapple flesh-side up, on a rack in a large grill pan. Place the pan as close as possible to the heat and grill for about 5 to 7 minutes until the fruit is browned and bubbly. Remove the fruit to a dish and keep warm.

■ Arrange the turkey cutlets on the grill rack. Place as close as possible to the heat and grill the turkey for 5 to 7 minutes, brushing frequently with marmalade-spice mixture and turning the cutlets once, until the turkey just loses its pink colour throughout.

DUCK WITH GINGER SAUCE

───── VIETNAM ─────

SERVES 4

450 g/1lb Ho Chi Minh
  duck (see right)
vegetable oil for frying
12 thin slices root ginger,
  peeled and shredded
1½ tbsp hot soya paste
1½ tbsp sweet soya paste
  or hoisin sauce
1½ tsp rice wine
1½ tbsp Nuoc Mam sauce
  (optional)
1 tsp finely chopped garlic
1 tbsp chilli oil
1 tsp sugar
salt
225 ml/8 fl oz chicken
  stock
1 spring onion, shredded
1 red chilli pepper, fresh
  and shredded, or dried
  and crumbled
2 tsp cornflour mixed with
  a little water

HO CHI MINH DUCK
salt
pinch of five-spice powder
½ tsp finely chopped root
  ginger
½ tsp finely chopped garlic
½ tsp hot soya paste
1 oven-ready duck, about
  1.75–2 kg/4–4½ lb
125 ml/4 fl oz hot water
3 tbsp wine vinegar
20 g/¾ oz sugar
red food colouring

■ Make the Ho Chi Minh duck by mixing the salt, five-spice powder, ginger, garlic and soya paste. Put the mixture inside the duck's cavity and sew up both ends. Mix the remaining ingredients well and brush over the entire surface with a pastry brush. Leave to dry on a rack with the breast uppermost for 7 hours in a cool, dry place.

■ Preheat the oven to 200°C/400°F/Gas Mark 6. Put the rack together with the duck in a roasting tin and roast for 1 hour. Reduce the heat if the skin begins to burn. (Ideally, the duck should be roasted upright in the Oriental style but most household ovens cannot accommodate an upright duck. Laying it on its back is the next best thing.)

■ Take the cooked duck meat off the bone in as large pieces as possible and cut these into neat pieces about 1 x 2.5 cm/½ x 1 in. Heat the oil in a wok until it starts smoking and stir-fry the duck pieces for a few minutes. Set these aside, making sure to drain well.

■ Empty and wipe the wok, heat some more oil in it and stir-fry the ginger very briskly; add the soya bean pastes, return the duck to the wok and stir in the rice wine, Nuoc Mam sauce, if used, garlic, chilli oil, sugar and salt. Stir-fry for a few more minutes.

■ Add the chicken stock to the wok. As soon as it comes to the boil, reduce the heat and simmer, uncovered, for 5 minutes. Increase the heat, add the spring onions and chilli and cook fast for 1 minute, then stir in the cornflour.

BEEF

LIVER WITH MINT

LEBANON

This is an unusual combination of flavours, but is exquisite.
If fresh mint is not available, half the quantity of dried mint can be used.

SERVES 4

15 g/½ oz butter
1 tbsp olive oil
1 onion, finely sliced
1 garlic clove, crushed
450 g/1 lb calves' or
   lambs' liver, very thinly
   sliced

flour for dredging
125 ml/4 fl oz red wine
   vinegar
2 tbsp very finely chopped
   fresh mint

■ Heat half the butter and oil over medium-high heat. Sauté the onion until it is limp, add the garlic and continue cooking until the onion is lightly coloured. Remove the onion and garlic with a slotted spoon and reserve.

■ Quickly dredge the liver in the flour and shake off the excess. Add the remaining butter and oil to the pan and sauté the liver slices quickly on both sides. Return the onions and garlic to the pan, pour in the vinegar and stir in the mint. Cook for about 5 minutes, spooning the sauce over the liver, until the liquid is reduced and glazes the meat.

MEATLOAF

POLAND

*A very simple meat roll to serve with boiled potatoes
and red cabbage with onion and apple.*

SERVES 6

1 dried mushroom or 1
  tbsp mushroom ketchup
700 g/1½ lb minced veal
40 g/1½ oz fresh
  breadcrumbs
2 tbsp chopped fresh
  parsley

2 tbsp chopped fresh dill
  (optional)
salt and freshly ground
  black pepper
1 egg, beaten
a little oil to brush

■ Simmer the dried mushroom, if used, in just enough water to cover for 5 minutes. Drain and chop. Boil the cooking liquid until reduced to 1 tablespoon.

■ Mix the mushroom and cooking liquid or ketchup with all the remaining ingredients, pounding the meat mixture until smooth. Everything should be thoroughly combined. Grease a roasting tin. Set the oven at 180°C/350°F/Gas Mark 4.

■ Shape the meat mixture into a 20-cm/8-in long roll. Place it in the roasting tin and brush all over with oil. Bake for 1 hour, until lightly browned, firm and cooked through. Cut into slices to serve.

SPICY BEEF STEW

VIETNAM

SERVES 4

3 tbsp vegetable oil
2 medium onions, finely chopped
5 garlic cloves, finely chopped
10 spring onions, dead skin peeled off
1 stalk lemon grass, cut into 5-cm/2-in sections and crushed
900 g/2 lb stewing beef, cut into 2.5-cm/1-in cubes

1.2 ltr/2 pt water
90 ml/3½ fl oz yellow bean sauce, chopped and crushed
1 tsp chilli powder
4 star anise
2.5 cm/1 in cinnamon stick
½ tsp whole peppercorns
sugar

■ Heat 1 tablespoon oil in a wok over a medium-high heat. Put in the onions, garlic and whole spring onions and stir-fry for 2 minutes. Add the lemon grass and continue to stir until the onions become lightly brown. Remove the spring onions and set aside.

■ Heat the remaining oil over a high heat. Stir-fry as many pieces of beef as are convenient until they are brown, turning them over from time to time. Continue until all the beef has been cooked.

■ Add the water, the lemon grass mixture, yellow bean sauce, chilli powder, star anise, cinnamon, peppercorns and sugar and bring to the boil. Cover and lower the heat to simmer gently for 1½ hours.

■ Add the reserved spring onions; cover again and allow to simmer for a further 15 minutes, or until the sauce has thickened a little and the meat is tender.

STEAK WITH ANCHOVIES AND OLIVES

ITALY

Pasta or a classic, creamy risotto are ideal accompaniments for this Italian-style steak stir-fry.

SERVES 4

700 g/1½ lb frying steak, cut into strips
1 garlic clove, crushed
2 tbsp tomato purée
225 ml/8 fl oz red wine
salt and freshly ground black pepper
4 tbsp plain flour
4 tbsp olive oil
1 onion, halved and thinly sliced

1 green pepper, halved, seeded and thinly sliced
50-g/2-oz can anchovy fillets, drained and chopped
125 g/4 oz black olives, stoned and sliced
2 tbsp chopped parsley
handful of basil leaves, coarsely shredded

■ Place the steak in a dish. Mix the garlic, tomato purée and wine with seasoning, then pour the mixture over the steak. Mix well, cover and leave the meat to marinate overnight.

■ Drain the steak, reserving the marinade. Pat the strips of meat dry on kitchen paper, then toss them in the flour.

■ Heat 3 tablespoons of the olive oil, then stir-fry the onion and pepper for 5 minutes. Add the steak and stir-fry over fairly high heat until the strips are evenly browned. Pour in the reserved marinade and stir until the sauce boils. Simmer for 5 minutes, stirring, then taste for seasoning before transferring the meat mixture to a serving dish.

■ Wipe out the pan and heat the remaining olive oil. Add the anchovies, olives and parsley and toss them in the hot oil for 30 seconds. Stir in the basil, then pour the mixture over the steak and serve at once.

COOK'S TIP

For a milder, less salty result, the anchovy fillets may be drained, soaked in a little milk for 5 minutes, then drained again.

MEATBALLS WITH FRESH TOMATO SAUCE

——— POLAND ———

*These meatballs are extremely versatile. Serve them with almost
any sauce and accompany with noodles, rice or potatoes.*

SERVES 4

450 g/1 lb minced veal
25 g/1 oz fresh white
  breadcrumbs
1 egg, beaten
1 tsp dried marjoram
salt and freshly ground
  black pepper
600 ml/1 pt veal or
  chicken stock

TOMATO SAUCE
1 onion, chopped
25 g/1 oz butter
1 bay leaf
1 kg/2¼ lb tomatoes,
  roughly chopped
large parsley sprig
1 tsp sugar
1 tsp cider vinegar
150 ml/¼ pt soured cream

■ Mix the veal, breadcrumbs, egg, marjoram and
seasoning, then pound them together until thoroughly
combined. Wet your hands and shape the mixture into
16 meatballs about the size of large plums. Make sure
they are all nicely smooth.

■ Heat the stock in a saucepan until just simmering.
Add the meatballs, cover and simmer for 25 minutes.
Drain the meatballs, reserving the stock. Set aside,
covered, while making the sauce.

■ For the sauce, cook the onion in the butter with the
bay leaf in a pan for 10 minutes, until soft. Add the
tomatoes, parsley and reserved stock. Bring to the boil,
reduce the heat and simmer steadily, uncovered, for 1
hour. Press the sauce through a sieve and return it to
the rinsed pan. Add the sugar and vinegar, seasoning to
taste and bring to the boil. Add the meatballs and
simmer for 10 minutes, or until heated through. Stir in
the soured cream; heat very gently without boiling for
about 1 minute. Serve at once.

CARNE CON CHILE COLORADO

MEXICO

Rather than being a mixture of cheap minced beef, beans and tomato sauce, this recipe consists of large chunks of tender meat in a thick, smooth, rich sauce.

SERVES 4

8 middle-sized dried
  chillies: California or
  New Mexico type,
  deseeded and deveined
½ tsp cumin seeds
3 garlic cloves, peeled
1 small onion, chopped

1 tsp dried oregano
700 g/1½ lb lean,
  boneless beef or pork
oil or lard for frying
450 ml/¾ pt water or
  stock
salt to taste

■ Tear the chillies into reasonably flat pieces, then toast them briefly in a hot, dry frying pan. Hold them down for a few seconds until they change colour and crackle. Repeat on the other side. Do not allow them to burn or they will become bitter. Transfer them to a bowl and cover with boiling water. Place a saucer on top to keep them submerged and leave to soak at least 30 minutes. While they are soaking, grind the cumin seeds in a pestle and mortar or spice grinder.

■ Drain the chillies, but keep 225 ml/8 fl oz of the soaking liquid. Add the garlic, onion, oregano and fresh-ground cumin. Purée the lot, with the soaking liquid, in a blender. Blend until smooth, then strain through a wire sieve: this is one of the most time-consuming parts, but it makes for a wonderfully smooth sauce.

■ Cut the meat into approximately 2.5-cm/1-in cubes, and fry in a heavy, deep frying pan with a little lard or oil until browned all over – about 10 minutes. Keep turning the meat and scraping the pan.

■ Add the strained sauce; continue to cook, stirring and scraping frequently to avoid burning, for a few minutes (5 at most). The purée should be thick and rather darker than when you started. Add the water or stock; bring to a boil, and simmer over a low heat for at least an hour, stirring occasionally. If the sauce gets too thick, add a little more water or stock. It is ready when the meat is *very* tender.

BEEF **E**NCHILADAS WITH **R**ED **C**HILLI **S**AUCE

MEXICO

Enchiladas, one of Mexico's most popular dishes, are a combination of meat, cheese and sauce rolled up in a soft tortilla and baked. Barbecued meat gives them extra flavour, but any cooked and shredded beef will do. To counteract the heat of the Red Chilli Sauce, serve soured cream or yoghurt on the side.

SERVES 6

375 g/13 oz cooked
   beef, shredded
75 g/3 oz spring onions,
   chopped
450 g/1 lb grated
   Cheddar cheese
oil for frying
12 corn tortillas
soured cream or plain
   yoghurt

RED CHILLI SAUCE
12 dried New Mexico
   chillies
600 ml/1 pt beef stock
4 garlic cloves, crushed
75 g/3 oz chopped onion
½ tsp dried oregano
¼ tsp salt

■ First make the chilli sauce. Preheat the oven to 120°C/250°F/Gas Mark ½. Place the chillies on an ungreased baking sheet and bake for 6 to 8 minutes, shaking once or twice, until they are brittle. Do not allow them to blacken or they will be bitter. Remove the chillies and let stand until they are cool enough to handle. Remove the stems and as many of the seeds as desired.

■ Bring 1 ltr/1¾ pt water to the boil in a medium saucepan. Crumble the chillies into the boiling water and simmer for 20 to 30 minutes until soft. Drain off the water and discard. Purée the chillies in a food processor with about 6 tablespoons of the beef stock. Strain to remove the skins. Put the skins back in the food processor with another 6 tablespoons beef stock. Purée again and strain. Discard the skins.

■ Add the remaining sauce ingredients to the strained mixture and purée. Return the sauce to the heat, and simmer until it reaches the desired consistency.

■ Preheat the oven to 180°C/350°F/Gas Mark 4. Have ready a large, shallow baking dish, about 33 x 23 cm/ 13 x 9 in.

■ Mix together the beef, spring onions and sauce. Pour the remaining sauce into a wide, shallow dish.

■ The next stage is to fry the tortillas, dip them in red sauce, fill them with the beef mixture and the cheese, roll them up, and place them in the baking dish. Set up the utensils and ingredients so you can do this like an assembly line.

■ Pour oil into a frying pan to a depth of 5 mm/¼ in. Heat until hot, but not smoking, then add the first tortilla. Fry the tortilla just long enough to heat and soften it, 2 to 3 seconds per side. Hold the tortilla just above the pan for a few moments so excess oil can drain off. The heat under the pan should be high enough to reheat the oil after each tortilla, but not so high that it overheats and smokes while you are assembling each enchilada.

■ Working quickly, dip the tortilla in the sauce so both sides are immersed. Remove the tortilla and let excess sauce drip back into the dish. Lay the tortilla flat. Spread 3 tablespoons of the beef mixture in a thin line up the centre of the tortilla, then sprinkle 2 to 3 tablespoons of grated cheese over the beef. Tightly roll the enchilada into a cylinder and put it, seam-side down, in the baking dish. Repeat the process with the remaining tortillas and beef, squeezing the enchiladas into a single layer in the baking dish, if possible.

■ Spoon the remaining sauce over the enchiladas, then sprinkle the remaining cheese over. Bake, uncovered, for 15 minutes. Serve immediately, with soured cream or yoghurt.

PLANTAIN **R**INGS WITH **M**INCED **B**EEF

PUERTO RICO

SERVES 4

2 big, ripe plantains
50 g/2 oz butter or
 margarine
2 tsp vegetable oil
2 tbsp vegetable oil mixed
 with 1 tsp liquid annatto
450 g/1 lb lean minced
 beef
1 small onion, chopped
½ green pepper, chopped
1 fresh hot pepper,
 chopped

1 garlic clove, crushed
15 g/½ oz plain flour
2 ripe tomatoes, skinned
 and chopped
3 tbsp water
1 tsp salt
freshly ground black
 pepper
1½ tbsp vinegar
4 eggs
vegetable oil for frying

COOK'S TIP

*To peel plantains, cut off the ends then halve the plantain
across the middle with a sharp knife. Make 4 evenly
spaced lengthways slits in the skin of each half, cutting
through to the flesh from one end to the other. Peel away
the skin, one strip at a time.*

■ Peel the plantains (see Cook's Tip). Heat the butter
or margarine with the oil in a large frying pan. Cut each
plantain lengthways into 4 thick slices. Cook them in
the pan for 4 minutes, turning them over now and again
until they have browned. Drain them on kitchen paper.

■ Heat the annatto-flavoured oil in the same pan over
a medium heat and add the beef, onion, green pepper,
hot pepper and garlic. Cook for 5 minutes. Stir in the
flour, then add the tomatoes, water, salt and freshly
ground black pepper to taste. Cook until the mixture
thickens. Stir in the vinegar.

■ To make plantain rings, carefully bend each plantain
slice into a circle about 7.5 cm/3 in in diameter,
securing the overlapping ends with a wooden cocktail
stick. Lay the rings side by side.

■ Spoon the beef mixture into each ring and press the
tops as flat as possible. Beat the eggs and brush over
the filled rings.

■ Heat enough oil in a large pan to deep-fry the rings.
Fry them for about 3 minutes each side, turning them
over very gently. Drain on kitchen paper and serve as
soon as they are all cooked. Serve with rice 'n' peas.

BEEF **S**TROGANOFF

RUSSIA

SERVES 6 – 8

1 tbsp dry mustard powder
1 tbsp sugar
6 tbsp sunflower oil
3 large onions, sliced
450 g/1 lb fresh button or
    field mushrooms, sliced
1.25 kg/2½ lb fresh beef
    fillet, cut into 1-cm/½-in
    wide strips

salt and freshly ground
    black pepper
600 ml/1 pt sour cream
6 fresh parsley sprigs,
    stems removed, chopped
deep-fried straw potatoes
    (optional)

■ Combine the mustard and sugar in a bowl with water to make a paste. Let the flavours mingle while completing the recipe.

■ Heat half the sunflower oil in a large, heavy-bottomed shallow casserole. When just crackling, add the onions, reduce the heat to low, and stir. Gently soften the onions, covered, for about 25 minutes, stirring occasionally. During the last 10 minutes, uncover and add the mushrooms. Remove from the heat, drain the mixture, and set aside in a bowl.

■ Heat the remaining oil in the casserole. Drop in half the meat, stirring with a wooden spoon and turning the strips over to brown evenly. Transfer with a slotted spoon to the bowl with the vegetables; sauté the remaining meat. When all is browned, return the meat and vegetables to the casserole, together with the mustard mixture. Season to taste and add the sour cream, a little at a time, stirring continuously. Cover the casserole, heat through gently for about 5 minutes, and serve. Top each serving with a light scattering of parsley, and the straw potatoes, if desired.

BEEF IN **O**YSTER **S**AUCE

CHINA

SERVES 4

450 g/1 lb frying steak,
    cut into small, thin slices
3 tbsp oyster sauce
2 tbsp soy sauce
1 garlic clove, crushed
4 tbsp dry sherry
4 large dried Chinese

mushrooms
4 tbsp oil
1 green pepper, seeded
    and cut into chunks
1 red pepper, seeded and
    cut into chunks
1 onion, cut into chunks

■ Place the meat in a dish. Mix the oyster sauce, soy sauce, garlic and sherry together, then pour the mixture over the meat and mix well. Cover and leave to marinate for 2 to 4 hours. Place the mushrooms in a small basin or mug and pour in just enough hot water to cover them. Place a saucer or the base of another mug on the mushrooms to keep them submerged, then leave to soak for 20 minutes. Drain, reserving the soaking liquid, discard tough stalks and slice the mushroom caps.

■ Heat the oil, then stir-fry the peppers and onion for 3 minutes. Use a slotted spoon to add the beef to the pan, then continue stir-frying until the meat is cooked and lightly browned. Add the mushrooms.

■ Pour the soaking liquid into the oyster sauce marinade left from the meat and mix well, then pour the liquid into the pan. Bring to the boil and boil rapidly for a few minutes so that the meat is coated in a slightly thickened sauce. Serve at once with plain cooked rice or chow mein.

CHOLENT

ISRAEL

*Cholent is a long-simmering stew cooked on Friday
night and served at noon after the Sabbath morning service. It has
probably been made since Biblical times and is found in all Jewish
communities, but with slightly differing ingredients and flavourings;
the common essentials are meat and beans. The long, slow cooking
helps to tenderize an economical cut of meat.
A cholent, meaning 'hot-slow' in French, is made by every Ashkenazic
Jewish family and is really a layered hotpot that can include meat,
chicken, beans, sausages, dumplings and potatoes. Its counterpart is
found in the Sephardic dfina, which is prepared all over the Middle
East. This is a typical Ashkenazic version and contains a special
dumpling called a cholent knaidle.*

SERVES 8–10

2 tbsp vegetable oil
4 onions, sliced
4 garlic cloves, peeled
   and finely chopped
1.5 kg/3 lb boneless
   flank, brisket or beef
   shoulder, cubed
400 g/14 oz dried butter
   or red kidney beans,
   soaked at least 8 hours
200 g/7 oz pot barley
10–12 medium potatoes,
   peeled and halved
2 tsp salt
freshly ground black
   pepper
1½ tsp dried thyme

1 tsp paprika
2 bay leaves
2 tbsp sugar
50 ml/2 fl oz cold water

CHOLENT KNAIDLE
175 g/6 oz plain flour
¾ tsp baking powder
½ tsp salt
freshly ground black
   pepper
175 g/6 oz chicken fat, or
   margarine, finely
   chopped
2 tbsp chopped fresh
   parsley
4–6 tbsp cold water

■ In a large ovenproof casserole with tight-fitting lid, over medium-high heat, heat oil. Add onions and cook until well browned, 7 to 10 minutes. Stir in garlic and cook 1 minute longer. Remove to a plate and set aside.

■ Into same casserole, add meat and cook on all sides until pieces are well browned, 7 to 10 minutes. Remove meat to another plate and remove casserole from heat, leaving any remaining oil.

■ Return onions and garlic to casserole, spreading them evenly over bottom. Drain beans and add them, then layer in beef cubes, barley and potatoes, sprinkling salt, pepper to taste, thyme and paprika between layers. Tuck in bay leaves.

■ In a small saucepan, over high heat, bring sugar to a boil with 2 tablespoons water. Cook until sugar turns a dark caramel colour, 1 to 2 minutes. Off the heat and holding pan away from you, carefully pour in the water (caramel will splatter). Return to heat to liquidize caramel, then pour into casserole.

■ Pour in enough water to cover all layers and, over high heat, bring to a boil. Skim off any foam which comes to the surface. Lower heat and cook 30 minutes. Add a little more water if necessary.

■ Prepare knaidle. Preheat oven to 100°C/200°F/Gas Mark ¼ or lowest setting. Into a medium bowl, sift flour, baking powder, salt and pepper to taste. Cut in chicken fat or margarine. Add chopped parsley and cold water, then stir to form a soft dough. Form into large dumpling or a sausage shape.

■ Remove casserole from heat. Gently place knaidle on top of ingredients in the casserole, tucking it in gently. Cover tightly and cook in the very low oven 10 to 12 hours or overnight. Serve cholent from the casserole.

GREEK HAMBURGERS

GREECE

*Greek hamburgers can be served hot or cold, but they should
never be overcooked.*

SERVES 6–8

450 g/1 lb minced beef
2 slices of bread, crusts
    removed
2 tbsp milk
3 tbsp olive oil
50 g/2 oz butter
1 small onion, finely
    chopped
1 garlic clove, crushed
1 small carrot, finely
    grated

1 tomato, skinned and
    chopped
4 tbsp chopped fresh
    parsley
2 tbsp red wine
salt and freshly ground
    black pepper, to taste
225 g/8 oz plain flour

■ Place the beef in a large mixing bowl. Place the
bread on a plate and sprinkle over the milk. Allow to
soak for 5 minutes, or until the milk has been absorbed,
then add to the minced beef. Mix well to combine. Set
aside for the time being.

■ Heat 1 tablespoon of the olive oil and 15 g/½ oz of
the butter in a frying pan until the butter has melted.
Add the onion, garlic, carrot and tomato and sauté for
about 7 minutes, or until the onion has browned. Add
the sautéed vegetables to the meat mixture with the
parsley, wine and salt and freshly ground black pepper.
Mix thoroughly. Set aside for about 30 minutes.
■ Sprinkle the flour evenly over a baking sheet. Using
slightly damp hands, shape the meat mixture into
burger shapes, then drop them into the flour and coat
on both sides. Place the coated burgers on a clean
baking sheet lined with greaseproof paper.
■ Heat the remaining olive oil and butter in a large
frying pan until sizzling. Fry the burgers in batches,
cooking for about 5 minutes on each side, taking care
when turning them over. Add a little extra olive oil and
butter as you cook the batches if necessary. Transfer the
cooked burgers to a warm plate while you cook the
remaining burgers. Serve warm or cold.

S TEAK T ARTARE

RUSSIA

According to legend, Steak Tartare – one of the most renowned dishes to come out of Russia – was discovered by the fabled horsemen-warriors of Tartary. Always on the warpath, and with little or no time to cook their food, they tenderized meat under their saddles to make it palatable raw. In expensive Russian and East European restaurants, Steak Tartare is always a first course; in the West it is usually served as an entrée.

S ERVES 4

2 large egg yolks
3 spring onions, finely chopped
2 tsp Dijon-style mustard
1 tbsp Worcestershire sauce
1 tbsp bottled horseradish sauce
1 tbsp vegetable oil
2 tsp pepper vodka
1 tbsp finely chopped capers

450 g/1 lb fillet of beef, minced three times
salt and freshly ground black pepper

GARNISH
watercress sprigs
radishes, trimmed and scrubbed
spring onions, trimmed

■ Beat the eggs in a large bowl. One after the other, stir in the onions, mustard, Worcestershire sauce, horseradish, oil, vodka and capers. With your hands, gently work the beef into the mixture and season to taste. Form into 4 patties and arrange on a serving dish. Garnish attractively with the watercress, radishes and spring onions.

R OPAS V IEJAS

CUBA

In Spanish, the literal translation is 'old clothes' because, frankly, that's how drab a pile of shredded beef looks. This dish looks smashing, though, especially if tucked inside warmed flour tortillas and garnished with pimentos.

S ERVES 4 – 6

900 g/2 lb skirt or flank steak
1 large onion, halved
4 garlic cloves, finely chopped
1 large celery stalk, chopped
salt and freshly ground black pepper
4 tbsp olive oil
1 large onion, thinly sliced
1 large green pepper, seeded and cut into thin strips

3 large ripe tomatoes, finely diced
125 ml/4 fl oz dry white wine, or 2 tbsp dry sherry
2 bay leaves
2 tbsp ground cumin
25 g/1 oz cooked mange tout at room temperature (optional)
50 g/2 oz canned pimentos, drained and chopped for garnish (optional)

■ Place the steak in a large stockpot and add water to cover completely. Add halved onion, half the garlic, the celery and 1 tablespoon salt and bring to a boil. Cover, reduce heat to moderate and cook until meat is tender, about 1¼ hours. Transfer meat to a plate, leave to cool, then cover and refrigerate until chilled. Shred chilled meat with your fingers and set aside. If it doesn't shred easily, pound it between sheets of greaseproof paper and it should easily pull apart.

■ In a large frying pan, heat olive oil. Add remaining garlic and cook over high heat until lightly browned, about 1 minute. Reduce heat to moderate and stir in sliced onion and green pepper. Cook, stirring occasionally, until softened, about 10 minutes.

■ Stir in tomatoes, wine or sherry, bay leaves, cumin and a pinch of salt. Increase the heat to moderately high and cook, stirring occasionally, about 25 minutes. Remove bay leaves. Add shredded meat, stir, and cook about 5 minutes, until meat is heated. Stir in mange tout, if desired, and remove from heat. Season with salt and pepper. Garnish, if desired, and serve immediately.

MEXICAN BEEF TZIMMES

MEXICO

*Tzimmes is a slowly cooked casserole of meat,
sweet vegetables, such as carrots or sweet potatoes, and fruit, most
often prunes. This version of it was devised by an elderly German-
Jewish cook in Mexico City. It combines old-world tradition with
new-world ingredients.*

SERVES 8

1.6 kg/3½ lb boneless
beef brisket
1½ tbsp plain flour
4–6 tbsp chicken fat or
vegetable oil
2 onions, thinly sliced
2–4 garlic cloves, peeled
2 x 400-g/14-oz cans
tomatoes
1 large mango, peeled
and flesh puréed
1 tsp salt
½ tsp dried red pepper
flakes, or to taste
1 tsp chilli powder
1 cinnamon stick

2 bay leaves
4 tbsp honey
4 carrots, sliced
2 large sweet potatoes or
yams, peeled and cut
into chunks
200 g/7 oz pitted prunes,
soaked in hot water for
2 hours and well
drained
2 x 400-g/14-oz cans red
kidney beans, rinsed
and drained
4 tbsp chopped fresh
coriander

■ Rinse beef under cold running water; dry well with
kitchen paper. Dredge meat with flour on both sides.

■ In a large casserole with tight-fitting lid, over
medium-high heat, heat 2 to 3 tablespoons chicken fat
or oil. Add beef and cook until underside is well
browned, 5 to 7 minutes. Turn beef and cook until
second side is well browned, 4 to 5 minutes longer.
Remove to a plate and set aside.

■ Add remaining chicken fat or oil and onions. Cook
until onion is softened and beginning to colour, 3 to 5
minutes. Stir in garlic and cook 1 minute longer. Pour in
tomatoes and their juice, stirring and scrape up any
meat juices. Add mango purée, salt, red pepper flakes,
chilli powder, cinnamon stick, bay leaves and honey
and cook, stirring often, 2 to 3 minutes.

■ Return beef to casserole and pour in enough water
to just cover meat. Cover tightly and simmer, over
medium-low heat, 1½ hours. (Check from time to time
to see if there is enough water.) Add carrots, sweet
potato chunks, prunes and beans. Cover and cook, over
medium heat, 30 minutes longer, adding a little more
water if necessary.

■ Transfer meat to a deep serving platter. If liquid is
too thin, reduce over medium-high heat until slightly
thickened, 5 to 10 minutes. Spoon vegetables and
beans around beef. Pour sauce over meat and sprinkle
meat and vegetables with chopped coriander. Serve
meat cut into thin slices.

HAMBURGERS WITH SPICY TOMATO SAUCE

— UNITED STATES —

S ERVES 4

450 g/1 lb lean minced
  beef
1 onion, peeled and finely
  chopped
1 green pepper, seeded
2 tbsp fresh breadcrumbs
1 egg, lightly beaten
1 tsp Worcestershire sauce
salt and freshly ground
  pepper

SPICY TOMATO SAUCE
1 tsp oil
1 onion, peeled and finely
  chopped
1 chilli pepper seeded
  (optional)
1 garlic clove, crushed
1 carrot, scraped and
  grated
200 g/7 oz canned
  peeled tomatoes
150 ml/¼ pt stock or
  water
1 bay leaf
½ tsp oregano

■ Place the meat in a bowl with the finely chopped onion. Chop the pepper into very small dice. (If you prefer, both onion and pepper can be chopped in a blender.) Add the breadcrumbs. Mix in the beaten egg and add the Worcestershire sauce and seasoning.

■ Divide the mixture into 8 pieces and shape into rounds. A scone or pastry cutter is ideal for this purpose. Place on a tray in the refrigerator to chill while making the sauce.

■ To make the sauce heat the oil in a saucepan and cook the onion and chilli over a low heat for 4 minutes. Add the garlic and grated carrot. Stir well, then add remaining ingredients. Season well. Simmer for at least 20 minutes on a low heat.

■ Brush the beefburgers with oil and grill under a high heat for 4 minutes each side. If you like beef well cooked, give the burgers a further 3 minutes.

MADRAS BEEF CURRY

INDIA

Curries are best made in advance as the spicy flavour improves with reheating. Serve with pilau rice, mango chutney and poppadoms.

SERVES 4

6 tbsp vegetable oil	1 tsp tomato purée
2 large onions, peeled	600 ml/1 pt beef stock or
4 celery stalks, washed	water
700 g/1½ lb stewing steak	425 g/15 oz canned
1 tbsp flour	peeled tomatoes
½ tsp paprika	1 medium potato, peeled
½ tsp garam masala	
1–2 tbsp Madras curry	GARNISH
powder	onion rings
1 bay leaf	1 tbsp chopped parsley

■ Heat 4 tablespoons oil in a large frying pan. Cut off a few thin onion rings for garnish, then finely chop the remainder and cook for 5 minutes.

■ Remove the strings from the celery and chop finely. Add to the onions and stir well for a further 2 minutes. Remove to a casserole or thick-bottomed saucepan.

■ Trim the steak and remove any gristle. Cut into 2.5-cm/1-in cubes. Combine the flour, paprika and garam masala and sprinkle over the meat. Add remaining oil to the frying pan and fry the meat until golden on all sides. Remove with a slotted spoon to the casserole.

■ Sprinkle the curry powder and any remaining flour into the pan and simmer for 2 minutes. Add the tomato purée to the stock and pour into the pan, stirring well to remove meat juices. Add the canned tomatoes and bring to the boil. Meanwhile cut the potato into cubes and bring to the boil for 5 minutes in salted water.

■ Add the tomato and curry mixture to the meat and onions. Stir well. Drain the potato cubes and add to the casserole with ½ teaspoon salt. Cook in the oven for 1 hour or until the meat is tender. Taste and season accordingly.

COOK'S TIP

This curry can be cooked on top of the cooker, but remember to check from time to time that it is not sticking or drying out. Add a little stock or water if necessary.

SIMMERED BEEF WITH TURNIPS AND CARROTS

SPAIN

It is very typical to pot-roast or simmer joints of beef in Spain, where the quality of meat is generally not very good. Roasting is a method reserved for very young animals. This is an excellent dish of sliced meat, served with its own root vegetables.

SERVES 6

salt and freshly ground	4 carrots, thickly sliced
black pepper	4 small turnips, chopped
1–2 tbsp paprika	in eight
1.5 kg/3 lb beef rump,	2 sprigs of thyme
shoulder or shank, tied	4 parsley stalks, bruised,
in one piece	plus 2 tbsp chopped
2 tbsp lard	parsley
3 onions, chopped	1 sprig of mint
200 g/7 oz unsmoked	1 bay leaf
bacon, salt or fresh pork	150 ml/¼ pt red wine
belly, cubed	150 ml/¼ pt red wine
1 piece of bone, such as	vinegar
a bit of beef shin or	
gammon knuckle	

■ Rub salt, pepper and the paprika into the beef. Heat the lard in a deep casserole, which should be the right size to take everything neatly, and brown the meat on all sides. Then put the chopped onions round the meat and allow them to soften, adding the pork cubes and stirring occasionally.

■ Fit the bone, carrots, turnips and the herbs (preferably tied together with a bit of cotton) into the casserole. Then add a little more seasoning and the chopped parsley. Pour in the wine and vinegar and bring to simmering, uncovered. Fit a sheet of foil securely under the lid and simmer for 1½ hours very gently until the meat is cooked.

■ Transfer to a serving plate and let the meat rest for 10 minutes. Carve it into slices and arrange the vegetables and pork around it. Discard the bone and herbs. Blend the contents of the casserole and return to the pot to rewarm. Check the seasonings. Pour some gravy over the meat and serve the rest in a sauce boat.

PICADILLO

MEXICO

SERVES 4–6

900 g/2 lb lean beef
4 tbsp olive oil or lard
1 medium onion, sliced
2–4 garlic cloves, crushed
1 chayote, peeled and cubed
1 large potato, peeled and cubed
2 large tomatoes, cut in chunks
2 carrots, peeled and sliced

1 courgette, sliced
25 g/1 oz raisins
3 or more canned, sliced jalapeño chillies
10 pimento-stuffed olives, halved
large pinch each of cinnamon and cloves (about ⅛ tsp)
salt and pepper
175 g/6 oz peas
50 g/2 oz flaked

■ Cut the beef in strips, as described above, or chop finely. Heat the oil or lard in a heavy pan and fry the beef until brown; add the onions and garlic. When these are golden, add all the other ingredients except the peas and almonds. Bring to the boil; simmer for 20 to 30 minutes, according to how well done you like the vegetables. Five minutes (or less) before serving, stir in the peas.

■ Fry the almonds in a little olive oil (or almond oil), shaking the pan constantly to avoid burning. When they are golden-brown, sprinkle them over the picadillo.

BEEF WITH **L**EMON **G**RASS AND **M**USHROOMS

VIETNAM

SERVES 4

450 g/1 lb fillet steak, sliced very thinly across the grain and cut into 5 x 7.5-cm/2 x 3-in pieces
2 stalks fresh lemon grass, sliced paper-thin and finely chopped
2 fresh red chilli peppers, crushed
6 garlic cloves, crushed
3 tbsp Nuoc Mam sauce or light soy sauce
1 tsp arrowroot or cornflour

freshly ground black pepper
3½ tbsp vegetable oil
2 medium onions, finely sliced
125 g/4 oz button mushrooms
1 tsp sugar
50 g/2 oz roasted peanuts, coarsely ground
sprigs of coriander to garnish

■ Combine the beef, lemon grass, chilli, half the garlic, 2 tbsp Nuoc Mam sauce, arrowroot, black pepper and 2 tbsp oil in a bowl. Set aside for 30 minutes.

■ Pour 1 tablespoon of oil into a wok over a medium heat and add the onions and the remaining garlic. Stir-fry for 1 to 2 minutes until golden brown. Remove the onions and set aside. Heat ½ tablespoon more oil and, when hot, add the beef mixture, the mushrooms, the rest of the Nuoc Mam sauce and the sugar. Sauté over a high heat for 1 to 2 minutes, or until the beef is cooked.

■ Scoop the food from the wok and arrange it on a warmed serving dish. Arrange the sautéed onions around it and sprinkle the peanuts and black pepper over everything. Garnish with coriander sprigs.

GREEN BEEF CURRY

THAILAND

Definitely green, but rarely sweet, this is one of the basic Thai curry styles, and can be used with pork, chicken or duck as a variation from beef.

SERVES 4

CHILLI PASTE
1 tbsp sliced shallot
1 tbsp chopped garlic
1 tbsp sliced galangal
½ stalk of lemon grass, sliced
½ tbsp coriander seeds
2 tsp salt
1 tsp shrimp paste
½ tsp chopped kaffir lime zest
½ tsp chopped coriander root or stem
6 white peppercorns, crushed
20 fresh small green chillies, roughly chopped

1.25 ltr/2 pt thin coconut milk
325 g/11 oz beef sirloin, cut into 2.5 x 2 x 1-cm/ 1 x ¾ x ¼-in slices
2 tbsp fish sauce
½ tbsp palm sugar
10 small white aubergines, quartered
3 fresh red chillies, quartered lengthwise
3 kaffir lime leaves, torn into small pieces
15 g/½ oz sweet basil leaves

■ Pound all the chilli paste ingredients except the green chillies together to form a fine paste. (This can be done using a mortar and pestle or blender.) Stir in green chillies.

■ Heat 225 ml/8 fl oz of the coconut milk in a pan, add the chilli paste and cook for 2 minutes. Add the beef and the rest of the coconut milk, and bring to the boil. Add the fish sauce and palm sugar, boil for 2 more minutes, then add the aubergine and chilli and cook for 1 minute. Stir in the lime leaf, boil for 1 minute, add the basil and remove from the heat. Serve in bowls accompanied by rice, pickled vegetables and salted eggs.

BEEF IN COCONUT MILK

— VIETNAM —

SERVES 4

2 tbsp vegetable oil
1 garlic clove, crushed
225 g/8 oz topside of
  beef, thinly sliced
1 small onion, thinly sliced
pinch of turmeric
½ green chilli pepper
1 cm/½ in lemon grass,
  cut from the bottom,
  thinly sliced
1 tbsp canned coconut
  milk

GARNISH
1 tbsp peanuts, crushed
handful of fresh coriander,
  chopped

◼ Heat the oil until very hot. Add the garlic. When the smell is released, add everything except the coconut milk. Stir-fry for about 3 minutes or until the meat is cooked.

◼ Add the coconut milk and stir once. Serve garnished with crushed peanuts and chopped coriander.

BEEF AND ONION STEW

— GREECE —

SERVES 8–10

50 g/2 oz butter
1.5 kg/3 lb braising steak,
  cut into 5-cm/2-in cubes
300 ml/½ pt dry red wine
400-g/14-oz can chopped
  tomatoes
4 tbsp tomato purée
300 ml/½ pt boiling water
3 tbsp olive oil

3 onions, chopped
3 garlic cloves, crushed
1 tsp ground cinnamon
½ tsp dried oregano
salt and freshly ground
  black pepper, to taste
4 tbsp chopped fresh
  parsley, to garnish

◼ Melt the butter in a large, heavy saucepan and add the cubed meat. Stir and rearrange the meat to brown evenly on all sides.

◼ Add half the wine and simmer for 5 minutes. Stir in the chopped tomatoes, tomato purée and boiling water. Cover and simmer for 10 minutes.

◼ Meanwhile, heat the oil in a frying pan and cook the onions and garlic for about 5 minutes, or until browned. Transfer to the meat in the saucepan and add the cinnamon, oregano, salt and freshly ground black pepper. Cover the stew and simmer over gentle heat for 1 to 1½ hours or until the meat is very tender, adding the remaining wine during cooking. Sprinkle with chopped fresh parsley to serve.

STUFFED BEEF ROLLS

FRANCE

SERVES 4

	STUFFING
4 slices lean shoulder steak	25 g/1 oz butter
2 tbsp vegetable oil	1 small onion, peeled and
1 onion, peeled and sliced	thinly sliced
1 garlic clove, crushed	125 g/4 oz long-grain
1 tbsp flour	rice
1 bay leaf	salt and freshly ground
salt and freshly ground	pepper
pepper	pinch of saffron or a few
1 bouquet garni	drops of yellow food
1 sprig parsley	colouring
150 ml/¼ pt red wine	200 ml/7 fl oz stock
300 ml/½ pt beef stock	

■ First make the stuffing. Preheat the oven to 180°C/350°F/Gas Mark 4. Melt two thirds of the butter in a pan and cook the onion over a low heat for 4 minutes. Add the rice and continue stirring for another 3 minutes. Season well. Add the saffron or colouring to the stock. Then pour the stock on to the rice and mix well with a fork. Bring to the boil, transfer to a casserole with a lid and cook in the oven for about 15 minutes until stock is absorbed and rice grains are separate.

■ Lay the thin slices of beef on a board and trim off surplus fat. Cut into suitable sizes for rolls, about 7 cm/2½ in. Place 1 tablespoon rice stuffing on each slice. Roll tightly and secure with string or a wooden cocktail stick.

■ Heat the oil in a frying pan and brown the rolls on each side. Place in an ovenproof casserole. Keeping frying pan on lower heat, fry onion and garlic in remaining oil for 3 minutes. Sprinkle with flour and brown slightly. Add the bay leaf, seasoning, bouquet garni, parsley and red wine. Stir well, then add the stock. Cook for 5 minutes.

■ Pour the sauce from the frying pan on top of the rolls and cook in the oven for 1 to 1½ hours or until meat is tender. Remove bouquet garni and bay leaf. Serve with a crisp green vegetable, such as green beans, broccoli or a mixture of carrots and peas.

PORK AND HAM

STIR-FRIED PORK AND CELERY

VIETNAM

SERVES 4

2 tbsp vegetable oil
450 g/1 lb lean pork,
  sliced thinly and cut in
  2.5 x 4-cm/1 x 1½-in
  pieces
1 tbsp soy sauce
1 tsp sugar
225 g/8 oz button
  mushrooms

225 g/8 oz spring
  cabbage, cut in 5-cm/
  2-in slices with tougher
  stalks discarded
4 celery sticks, sliced thinly
1 tbsp Nuoc Mam sauce
  (optional)
3 tbsp chicken stock
cornflour
salt

■ Heat 1 tablespoon oil in a wok, add the pork and stir-fry over highest heat for 2½ minutes, or longer if the pork needs more cooking. Add the soy sauce and sugar and stir with the pork for a further 2 minutes. Scoop into a bowl and keep in a warm oven.

■ Wipe the wok and pour in the remaining oil. Add the mushrooms, cabbage and celery and stir-fry for 1½ minutes. Add the Nuoc Mam sauce, if using, and stock and stir-fry for another minute. Cover and leave to cook for a further 2 minutes. Then add the cooked pork with the cornflour and salt to taste. Stir for a minute or so and serve immediately with rice or noodles.

NASI GORENG

INDONESIA

SERVES 4

450 g/1 lb long-grain rice
salt
2 tbsp oil
2 medium onions, peeled
2 garlic cloves, crushed
2 fresh chilli peppers,
  seeded
1 tsp garam masala
2 tbsp soya sauce
½ tsp Worcestershire sauce
4 tbsp oil
125 g/4 oz cooked
  prawns

225 g/8 oz cooked, diced
  chicken
125 g/4 oz cooked, diced
  ham
3 eggs (or 4 if making the
  omelette)
salt and freshly ground
  pepper

GARNISH
1 tbsp chopped spring
  onions

■ Cook the rice in 1.2 ltr/2 pt boiling water with 1 teaspoon salt. Fork through the grains to make sure they are separated, then put on lid and simmer for at least 12 minutes.

■ Heat 2 tablespoons of oil in a frying pan. Add 1 finely chopped onion and the garlic, and cook until translucent. Remove with a slotted spoon.

■ In a blender or food processor whizz together the other chopped onion and chilli peppers, the garam masala, and the soya and Worcestershire sauces to make a paste. Add the remaining oil and fry the paste over a medium heat for about 3 minutes.

■ Add the prawns, chicken and ham and stir for a few minutes. Beat the eggs with salt and pepper. Turn the heat up fairly high and add the egg mixture, stirring continuously until the egg begins to set. Add the cooked rice and blend with the other ingredients on a lower heat.

VARIATION

If you like this garnished with omelette strips, use 4 eggs. Add 2 to the meat and prawn mixture, and use two for the omelette.

■ *For an omelette, take 2 eggs. Beat with a fork. Add seasoning. Melt a knob of butter in an omelette pan over a high heat. Pour in the egg mixture and pull the cooked edges back from the sides of the pan to the centre. When mixture is almost set, place the pan under a hot grill for about 1 minute. Cut into thin strips.*

■ *To serve, decorate the top of the rice dish with the omelette strips. Add a few chopped spring onions.*

FEIJOADA

—————— BRAZIL ——————

SERVES 6–8

350 g/12 oz dried black
  beans
450 g/1 lb pork loin, cut
  into 2-cm/¾-in cubes
salt and pepper to taste
2 tbsp fresh lemon juice
4 tbsp olive oil
450 g/1 lb linguica
  sausage, cut into
  1-cm/½-in slices

GARLIC SALSA
5 large tomatoes, peeled,
  seeded and diced
150 g/5 oz chopped
  onion
1 large jalapeño chilli,
  trimmed of all but a few
  seeds and veins
½–¾ tsp salt
20 garlic cloves, crushed
1½ tbsp chopped fresh
  basil or 1½ tsp dried

■ First make the garlic salsa. Simmer the tomatoes, onion, chilli and salt for about 15 minutes to evaporate excess liquid. Add the garlic and basil, and cook for another 2 to 3 minutes. Taste and adjust the salt if necessary. Set aside.

■ Pick through the beans for pebbles or other debris. Put the beans in a large saucepan with 1.75 litres/ 3 pints water. Let soak overnight, or bring the water to the boil, boil for 2 minutes, then remove from the heat, cover, and let soak for 1 hour.

■ Put the pork in a non-metallic bowl and sprinkle with salt and pepper. Combine half the garlic salsa with the lemon juice and 2 tablespoons olive oil, mix with the pork, and let it marinate for about 30 minutes. Drain the salsa, but do not discard. Heat the remaining oil in a large frying pan and add the pork. Cook until the cubes are lightly browned, 6 to 8 minutes. They do not have to be cooked thoroughly.

■ Drain and rinse the beans. Put them in a large stewpot and add enough water to cover the beans by 2.5 cm/1 in. Bring to the boil, then reduce the heat and simmer, uncovered. Check the beans occasionally and add a little more water if needed.

■ Add the pork, the salsa that was used for marinade, and the remaining salsa to the beans, together with the linguica. Cook until the beans are tender and the liquid has reduced to a thick sauce, 1 to 1½ hours. Taste and add more salt if necessary. Ladle into bowls and serve.

PORK AND ROSEMARY RAVIOLI

ITALY

Depending on where you are in Italy, ravioli may be square or round. Round filled pasta may also be referred to as agnolotti, *again according to regional preferences and traditions.*

SERVES 12

2 tbsp olive oil
1 onion, finely chopped
2 garlic cloves, crushed
4 juniper berries, crushed
1 tbsp chopped rosemary
½ tsp ground mace
350 g/12 oz lean minced pork
50 g/2 oz fresh white breadcrumbs
50 g/2 oz mushrooms, chopped
salt and freshly ground black pepper
2 eggs

PASTA DOUGH
350 g/12 oz plain flour
1 tsp salt
3 eggs
4 tbsp olive oil
1 tbsp water

WHITE WINE SAUCE
50 g/2 oz butter
1 small onion, finely chopped
1 bay leaf
2 parsley sprigs with long stalks
50 g/2 oz button mushrooms, thinly sliced
40 g/1½ oz plain flour
300 ml/½ pt dry white wine
150 ml/¼ pt chicken stock
salt and freshly ground white or black pepper
300 ml/½ pt single cream
2 tbsp chopped parsley
freshly grated Parmesan cheese, to serve

■ First make the pasta dough. Mix the flour and salt together in a large bowl. Make a well in the middle, then add the eggs, olive oil and water. Mix with a spoon, gradually working in the flour. When the mixture begins to bind into clumps, scrape the spoon clean and knead the dough together with your hands.

■ Press the dough into a ball and roll it around the bowl to leave the bowl completely clean of the mixture. Turn the dough out on a lightly floured, clean surface and knead it thoroughly until smooth. Keep the dough moving and adding the minimum of extra flour to prevent it sticking as you work. Wrap the dough in a polythene bag and leave it to rest for 15 to 30 minutes before rolling it out. Do not chill the dough as this will make it difficult to handle.

■ Now make the filling. Heat the oil in a saucepan. Add the onion, garlic and juniper berries. Cook, stirring, for 15 minutes, or until the onion is softened. Stir in the rosemary, mace, pork, breadcrumbs, mushrooms and plenty of seasoning. Add 1 egg and thoroughly mix the ingredients, pounding them with the back of the spoon. Beat the remaining egg.

■ Roll out half the pasta dough slightly larger than a 45-cm/18-in square. Use a 5-cm/2-in round cutter to stamp out circles of pasta, dipping the cutter in flour occasionally so that it cuts the dough cleanly. The best way to do this is to stamp all the circles close together in neat lines in the dough, then lift away the unwanted trimmings when the whole sheet is stamped into circles. You should have about 80 circles. Keep any unused circles covered with cling film while you fill the ravioli. Brush a circle of dough with egg, then place some of the meat mixture on it and cover with a second circle of dough. Pinch the edges of the dough together to seal in the filling. Fill all the ravioli, then roll out the remaining dough and make a second batch.

■ Cook the ravioli in a large saucepan of boiling water, allowing 15 minutes once the water has come back to the boil. Do this in batches if necessary, then drain the pasta.

■ Now make the sauce. Melt the butter in a saucepan. Add the onion, bay leaf and parsley, then cook, stirring often, for 15 minutes, until the onion is softened slightly but not browned. Stir in the mushrooms, then stir in the flour. Gradually stir in the white wine and stock, then bring to the boil. The sauce will be too thick at this stage. Cover the pan tightly and allow the sauce to cook very gently for 15 minutes.

■ Add seasoning and beat the sauce well. Remove the bay leaf and parsley sprigs. Stir in the cream and parsley and heat gently without boiling. Pour the sauce over the ravioli and serve with Parmesan cheese.

PORK WITH PERNOD

FRANCE

If you do not have any Pernod, substitute Greek ouzo or Turkish raki.
Rice or couscous will match the full flavour of this simple dish.

SERVES 4

700 g/1½ lb lean boneless
  pork, diced
2 sage sprigs
2 thyme sprigs
125 ml/4 fl oz Pernod or
  other aniseed liqueur
salt and freshly ground
  black pepper
2 tbsp olive oil
1 leek, thinly sliced

2 small carrots, diced
225 g/8 oz button
  mushrooms, sliced
225 ml/8 fl oz soured
  cream
8 large iceberg lettuce
  leaves
tarragon sprigs to garnish
  (optional)

■ Place the pork in a dish with the sage and thyme, then pour in the Pernod or other liqueur. Add some seasoning, mix well and cover. Leave to marinate for about 2 hours.

■ Heat the oil, then stir-fry the leek and carrots for 5 minutes. Use a slotted spoon to add the pork to the pan, with the herb sprigs. Reserve the marinade. Stir-fry the pork until lightly browned, then add the mushrooms and stir-fry for a further 2 to 3 minutes before pouring in the marinade.

■ Bring the juices to the boil, reduce the heat and pour in the cream. Heat for 1 minute but do not allow the cream to boil. Taste for seasoning.

■ Arrange the lettuce leaves on a serving platter and spoon the pork mixture into them. Garnish with tarragon, if liked, and serve at once.

BARBECUED ISLA BONITA PORK

CUBA

Island spices give this a taste of the tropics, even on a wintry day.

SERVES 4

½ tbsp ground ginger
½ tbsp ground cinnamon
½ tbsp grated nutmeg
½ tsp dry mustard
4 pork loin steaks,
   125–175 g/4–6 oz
   each, trimmed of fat

vegetable oil for
   barbecuing
pineapple wedges
   (optional)

■ In a small bowl, combine the ginger, cinnamon, nutmeg and dry mustard, and stir well. Pat pork dry with kitchen paper. Rub pork with spice mixture. Place in a shallow dish, cover and chill 30 minutes.

■ Coat barbecue rack with oil and place pork on it over medium-hot coals about 12.5 cm/5 in from heat. Cover and cook, turning occasionally, until meat thermometer registers 70°C/160°F, about 25 minutes. Cut into 1-cm/½-in thick slices. Garnish with pineapple, if desired.

PORK LOIN WITH APPLE PRESERVES

LITHUANIA

The accompanying preserve for this dish must be made at least 3 days ahead of time

SERVES 4

900 g/2 lb rolled pork
   loin
125 ml/4 fl oz lager

PRESERVE
75 ml/3 fl oz dry cider
175 g/6 oz light brown
   sugar
3 dessert apples, peeled,
   cored and chopped
1 small onion, finely
   chopped
juice and rind of ½ lemon
½ red pepper, cored,
   seeded and chopped
1 garlic clove, crushed
   and finely chopped

2 tbsp peeled, finely
   chopped fresh root
   ginger
large pinch cayenne
   pepper
¼ tsp salt

MARINADE
1 tbsp honey
1 tbsp finely chopped fresh
   marjoram
1 tsp juniper berries,
   crushed
1 garlic clove, crushed
¼ tsp dried black
   peppercorn

■ Make the preserve first. Bring the cider and brown sugar to the boil in a large saucepan; stir until the sugar dissolves. Add the remaining ingredients and bring to the boil again. Reduce the heat and simmer, stirring occasionally, until the mixture is reduced to about 450 ml/¾ pt.

■ Place the marinade ingredients in a large plastic bag. Add the pork loin and roll it around in the bag to coat it. Tie the bag shut and place on a dish in a cool place for 24 hours. Turn it occasionally.

■ Preheat the oven to 190°C/375°F/Gas Mark 5. Remove the pork from the bag and discard the marinade. Place the pork on a trivet over a roasting tin and roast until the meat is done, about 50 to 55 minutes. Transfer the meat to a dish and keep warm.

■ Skim the fat from the drippings in the tray and discard. Pour the lager into the tray and bring to the boil over high heat, mixing the drippings into the lager. Reduce the liquid until thickened. Pour into a sauceboat and serve with the pork and preserves.

SWEET-SOUR PORK BALLS

CHINA

SERVES 4

450 g/1 lb minced pork
1 tsp sesame oil
4 tbsp cornflour
1 egg
2 tbsp soy sauce
2 tbsp oil

SWEET AND SOUR SAUCE
1 tsp cornflour
4 tbsp dry sherry
4 tbsp soy sauce

3 tbsp tomato purée
4 tbsp demerara sugar
2 tbsp white wine vinegar
225-g/8-oz can pineapple chunks in syrup
1 large onion, cut in chunks
1 large green pepper, cut in chunks
2 carrots, cut in 2.5-cm/ 1-in strips

■ Pound the pork with the sesame oil until well mixed, then mix in the cornflour, egg and soy sauce in the same way. Have a plate ready to hold the pork balls. Wash, then wet your hands under cold water. Take small portions of the meat mixture, about the size of walnuts, and knead them into balls. Keep wetting your hands as this prevents the meat from sticking to them, and it gives the balls an even surface.

■ Before cooking the pork balls, start preparing the sauce. Blend the cornflour to a paste with 4 tablespoons water. Add the sherry and soy sauce, then stir in the tomato purée, sugar and vinegar. Drain the liquid from the pineapple into the mixture.
■ Heat the oil and stir fry the pork balls until evenly browned and cooked through. Use a slotted spoon to remove them from the pan.
■ Add the onion, pepper and carrots to the hot fat and stir-fry these ingredients for about 5 minutes, until slightly softened. Give the liquid sauce mixture a stir, then pour it into the pan and bring to the boil, stirring all the time. Stir in the pork balls and pineapple and cook, stirring over reduced heat for 3 to 4 minutes.

PORK FILLETS IN BRANDY CREAM SAUCE

AUSTRIA

SERVES 4

700 g/1½ lb pork fillet
1 tbsp flour
salt and freshly ground pepper
25 g/1 oz butter
2 tbsp oil
1 onion, peeled and finely chopped

2 tbsp brandy
¼ tsp nutmeg
150 ml/¼ pt single cream

GARNISH
1 lemon
1 bunch of watercress

■ Trim the pork fillets. Remove any gristle and fat. Cut into diagonal slices. Beat out to about 1 cm/½ in thick. Coat each slice evenly in seasoned flour.
■ Heat the butter and oil in a frying pan and cook the onions for 4 minutes. Remove on to a plate.
■ On a medium heat sauté the pork fillet slices for about 4 minutes each side until golden brown. Heat the brandy in a ladle and set alight. Pour on to the pork and allow to flambé. Transfer the pork to a warmed serving dish in a low oven.
■ Add nutmeg and single cream to the frying pan and stir over a low heat to combine the meat juices and cream. Pour the sauce over the meat. Serve with wild rice and a crisp green salad. Garnish with lemon wedges and watercress.

PORK AND WHEAT

GREECE

SERVES 8–10

50 ml/2 fl oz olive oil
900 g/2 lb lean pork fillet,
  cut into large pieces
salt and freshly ground
  black pepper, to taste
2–3 red chillies, seeded

and finely chopped
225 g/8 oz whole wheat
50 g/2 oz butter
2 onions, peeled and
  chopped
1 tsp ground cumin

■ Heat the oil in a large saucepan and add the pork, turning to brown evenly. Add enough water to cover the meat and slowly bring to the boil. Season with salt and freshly ground black pepper, add the chopped chillies, reduce the heat and simmer, covered, for about 2 hours, or until the meat is extremely tender.

■ Meanwhile, place the wheat in a medium-sized saucepan with enough water to cover it by 7.5 cm/3 in. Bring to the boil, stir and reduce the heat. Simmer, covered, for about 1½ hours, or until the wheat is tender. Remove from the heat and drain.

■ Melt the butter in a frying pan and sauté the onions until softened but not coloured. Set aside. Transfer the cooked pork to a chopping board. Using two forks, shred the meat into small pieces and place on a warm serving dish with the wheat. Stir to combine, then top with the sautéed onion and butter. Sprinkle over the cumin and serve with Greek yoghurt.

PORK WITH BEANS

POLAND

This easy and hearty winter meal is guaranteed to bring a glow to the face after a walk in even the worst of winter weather.

SERVES 4

2 rashers rindless smoked
  bacon, diced
1 garlic clove, crushed
1 leek, sliced
1 onion, thinly sliced
2 carrots, sliced
1 bay leaf
450 g/1 lb lean, boneless
  pork, cubed
225 g/8 oz dried butter
  beans, soaked overnight

1.25 ltr/2 pt water
salt and freshly ground
  black pepper
450 g/1 lb celeriac, diced
2 tbsp plain flour
4 tbsp soured cream
3 tbsp chopped fresh dill
  or 1 tsp dried dill

■ Cook the bacon and garlic in a large, heavy-based flameproof casserole until the fat runs. Add the leek, onion, carrots and bay leaf and cook for about 5 minutes, until the onion begins to soften. Stir in the pork and drained beans. Pour in the water and bring to the boil. Make sure that the beans are well covered with water, adding extra if necessary. Reduce the heat, cover and simmer for 30 minutes. Check to make sure that the beans do not dry up on the surface during cooking.

■ Add plenty of seasoning and stir in the celeriac. Continue to cook the stew, half uncovered so that excess liquid evaporates, for a further 30 minutes, or until the beans are cooked.

■ Stir the flour and soured cream into a smooth paste and add a little cooking liquid from the pot. Stir the paste into the stew and bring to the boil. Simmer for 3 minutes, add the dill and serve.

PORK WITH COURGETTES

MEXICO

This is a straightforward dish. In the original version, the ribs were chopped into small pieces; using the meatier English-cut ribs gives a similar flavour, but fewer awkward bits of bone. Soy sauce may not seem very Mexican, but it appears in an increasing number of Mexican dishes.

SERVES 4

900 g/2 lb English-cut
  spare ribs
6 courgettes, sliced
1 medium onion, sliced
2 medium tomatoes, sliced
2 green California chillies
  or 1 sweet red pepper

475 ml/16 fl oz meat
  stock
1 tbsp soy sauce
fat for frying
salt and pepper

■ Fry the ribs until they are golden and season to taste. Pour off excess fat. Add all the other ingredients, cover, and cook slowly for at least 1 hour – 2 hours is not too long. Serve with rice cooked with a little mild chilli powder to add colour and flavour. It also goes well with boiled or mashed potatoes, and sweet corn.

SATAY-FLAVOUR PORK

THAILAND

SERVES 4

450 g/1 lb lean boneless
  pork, cut in thin strips
2 tbsp lime or lemon juice
2 tbsp ground coriander
1 tsp ground ginger
1 garlic clove, crushed
salt and freshly ground
  black pepper
1 tsp sesame oil
4 tbsp ground nut oil
1 bunch spring onions,
  shredded

SAUCE
1 small onion, chopped
2 garlic cloves, crushed

juice of 1 lime or lemon
½ tsp chilli powder
4 tbsp tahini
4 tbsp crunchy peanut
  butter
2 tbsp soy sauce

SALAD
½ iceberg lettuce,
  shredded
½ cucumber, halved and
  thinly sliced

GARNISH
spring onion curls
lime or lemon wedges

■ Place the pork in a basin. Add the lime or lemon juice, coriander, ginger, garlic, seasoning and sesame oil. Stir well so that all the pieces of meat are coated in the seasoning mix. Cover and leave to marinate for several hours or overnight.

■ For the sauce, blend the onion, garlic, lime or lemon juice, chilli and tahini to a paste in a liquidizer or food processor. Stir 3 to 4 tablespoons boiling water into the peanut butter to soften it to a paste, then stir in the blended mixture and the soy sauce. Add a little extra boiling water if necessary to thin the sauce.

■ Arrange the lettuce and cucumber on a platter or individual plates. Add the spring onion curls. Heat the groundnut oil and stir-fry the pork until browned and cooked through. Add the shredded spring onions and stir-fry for another minute. Arrange the meat on the salad base.

■ Spoon a little peanut sauce over the meat and spring onions, then serve the rest separately.

PORK AND HOMINY STEW

MEXICO

SERVES 8

140 g/4½ oz chopped
  onion
4 tbsp vegetable oil
3 garlic cloves, crushed
1.75 ltr/3 pt chicken stock
450 g/1 lb pork neck
  bones
2 dried California chillies
3 tbsp flour
1 tsp salt

1 tsp dried mustard
2 tsp dried oregano
2 tsp ground cumin
½ tsp cayenne pepper
½ tsp black pepper
1.5 kg/3 lb pork loin or
  other pork cut, cut into
  bite-sized cubes
700 g/1½ lb canned
  hominy

■ In a large stockpot, sauté the onion in 1 tablespoon oil for 5 minutes. Add the garlic and cook for 1 minute longer, then add the chicken stock and neck bones. Note the level of the liquid, then add 475 ml/16 fl oz water. If the stock falls below that level during cooking, add more water. Bring the stew to the boil, reduce the heat, and simmer, uncovered, for 2 hours.

■ While the stew is simmering, cut the chillies in half and discard the seeds. Put the chillies in a small, heat-resistant bowl and pour 6 tablespoons boiling water over them. Let soak for 20 minutes, stirring once or twice to be sure all parts of chillies are softened. Purée the water and chillies in a blender, then add this purée to the simmering stew.

■ After the stew has simmered for 2 hours, remove it from the heat. Remove the pork bones. If you have time, let the stock and the bones cool for ease of handling. Skim the fat from the stock and return the stock to the hob. Take off any meat from the bones and add it to the stew. Discard the bones and fat.

■ Mix together the flour, salt, mustard, oregano, cumin, cayenne and black pepper. Toss the pork cubes in this seasoning mixture until evenly coated. Heat the remaining oil in a large frying pan and sauté the pork just until it is golden brown. Add the pork cubes to the stew, bring to the boil, then reduce the heat and simmer, covered, for 20 minutes. Add the hominy and simmer for 10 minutes longer.

■ Taste the stock and adjust the salt to taste. Ladle the stew into large bowls and serve.

PASTA CARBONARA

ITALY

SERVES 4

450 g/1 lb tagliatelle
50 g/2 oz butter
350 g/12 oz cooked
  ham, shredded
8 eggs
salt and freshly ground
  black pepper

150 ml/¼ pt single cream
plenty of chopped parsley
freshly grated Parmesan
  cheese, to serve

■ Cook the tagliatelle in a large pan of boiling salted water. Meanwhile, melt the butter in a large, heavy-bottomed or non-stick saucepan. Add the ham and cook for 2 minutes. Beat the eggs with seasoning and the cream. Reduce the heat under the pan, if necessary, then pour in the eggs and cook them gently, stirring all the time until they are creamy. Do not cook the eggs until they set and scramble and do not increase the heat to speed up the process or the carbonara will be spoilt.

■ Drain the pasta and tip into the half-set eggs. Mix well and serve at once, sprinkled with parsley. Offer Parmesan cheese with the pasta carbonara.

PORK CHOPS WITH CAPERS AND PEPPERS

SPAIN

Pork chops are Spain's commonest fare, cooked on la plancha, *a hot iron, or fried. This colourful pepper and caper mixture has just the right acidity to balance the bland meat.*

SERVES 4

3 tbsp olive oil
1 small onion, chopped
1 garlic clove, finely
  chopped
1 green pepper, seeded
  and chopped
1 red pepper, seeded and
  chopped

4 pork chops
1 tsp paprika
salt and freshly ground
  black pepper
3 tbsp pickled capers

■ Heat the oil in a big frying pan and cook the onion gently for 10 minutes. Add the garlic and chopped peppers and fry, stirring occasionally, until the onions are soft (about another 10 minutes).

■ Sprinkle the chops with paprika – standard practice in Spain, where paprika is the country's most important pepper and is used more than black pepper. Season with salt and pepper. Fry them in the pan, pushing the vegetables to the sides or piling them on top of the chops, until the chops are cooked and browned on both sides. Chop the capers roughly, stir into the peppers, and heat through.

PORK WITH CLAMS

PORTUGAL

SERVES 6

1 kg/2¼ lb boneless pork loin, cut into 2.5-cm/1-in pieces
2 garlic cloves, finely crushed
2 tbsp red pepper paste (see right)
300 ml/½ pt medium-bodied dry white wine
1 bay leaf
2 coriander sprigs
salt and pepper
40 g/1½ oz bacon fat

1 large onion, finely chopped
1 kg/2¼ lb clams, scrubbed and well washed

RED PEPPER PASTE
3 large red peppers, seeded and quartered lengthways
1 tbsp sea salt
2 garlic cloves
4 tbsp olive oil

■ First make the red pepper paste. Stir together the peppers and salt; then leave, uncovered, at room temperature for 24 hours.

■ Preheat the grill. Rinse the peppers well, drain and pat dry. Place, skin-side up, on a baking sheet. Grill until the skins are charred and blistered. Leave to cool slightly before peeling off the skins and discarding. Purée the garlic and peppers in a blender, pouring in the oil slowly. Any leftover paste can be kept in a covered glass jar in the refrigerator for 2 weeks.

■ Put the pork into a non-metallic bowl. Mix the garlic into the red pepper sauce and blend with the wine. Pour over the pork, add the herbs and seasoning, and stir gently together. Cover and refrigerate for 24 hours, turning the pork occasionally. Lift the pork from the marinade with a slotted spoon; reserve the marinade.

■ Heat the bacon fat in a large, heavy-based flameproof casserole and cook the pork until evenly browned. Remove. Cook the onion in the same fat until softened but not coloured.

■ Return the pork to the casserole, add the reserved marinade and bring to simmering point. Cover tightly and cook very gently for about 1 hour. Add the clams, cover and cook until the clams open, about 8 to 10 minutes; discard any that remain closed.

ALMOND-STUFFED PORK WITH SHERRY AND CREAM

SPAIN

It's possible that the English, who introduced dairy cows to the Balearic Islands, influenced this sauce, but it's more likely to be related to Arab dishes of birds simmered in milk.

SERVES 6

800 g/1¾ lb eye-of-pork loin (6–7 chop centre loin, boned, skinned and all flaps trimmed away)
salt and freshly ground black pepper
125 g/4 oz almonds, toasted
2 tbsp flour
1 tbsp lard or butter
1 tbsp olive oil
4 tbsp fino sherry or Montilla
8 spring onion bulbs or 4 shallots, chopped
475 ml/16 fl oz meat or chicken stock
125 ml/4 fl oz double cream
1–2 spring onions, finely chopped (optional)

■ Cut the pork almost through horizontally. Open it like a book and season both sides well. Chop the almonds coarsely (don't overprocess if using a blender or food processor) and sprinkle inside the meat. Shut the meat and tie it in half a dozen places with string.

■ Dust the pork with seasoned flour. Heat the fat and oil in a flameproof casserole that fits the joint neatly, then brown the outside of the meat. Douse it with the fino and allow this to reduce, spooning it over the meat.

■ Add the spring onions or shallots and fry them for a couple of minutes. Pour the stock round the base of the meat. Cover the pan tightly, first with foil, then the lid, and pot roast for 1 hour.

■ Remove the meat and let it rest in a warm place. Boil the juices to reduce by half. Stir in the cream and warm the sauce through. It is not traditional to blend the sauce, but you might like to do so if you prefer it smooth. Carve the meat and arrange the slices, overlapping, on a serving platter. Pour the sauce over. If you wish, a sprinkling of finely chopped spring onion tops gives it a touch of green.

PORK CHOW MEIN

CHINA

This version of chow mein uses Chinese five-spice powder which, even in small quantities, gives a very strong flavour.

SERVES 4

450 g/1 lb lean, boneless pork, cut into very thin 2.5–5-cm/1–2-in squares
2 tsp sesame oil
1 garlic clove
2 tbsp soy sauce
6 tbsp dry sherry
pinch of five-spice powder
2 tbsp cornflour
350 g/12 oz fresh Chinese egg noodles
2 tbsp oil
1 onion, halved and thinly sliced
1 green pepper, seeded, quartered lengthways and thinly sliced
200-g/7-oz can bamboo shoots, drained and sliced
150 ml/¼ pt chicken stock

■ Place the pork in a basin. Add the sesame oil, garlic, soy sauce and 2 tablespoons sherry. Mix in the five-spice powder, cover and leave to marinate for 2 hours.

■ Remove the pork from the marinade and reserve the liquid. Place the meat in a polythene bag, add the cornflour and shake the bag, holding it closed, to coat the meat evenly. Cook the noodles in boiling salted water for 3 minutes, then drain them, rinse under cold water and set aside.

■ Heat the oil in a wok or large frying pan. Add the pork and stir-fry over fairly high heat until the pieces are evenly and lightly browned. Stir in the onion and pepper and continue to stir-fry for 5 minutes, until the pork is well cooked and the vegetables are softened very slightly. Stir in the bamboo shoots.

■ Mix the remaining sherry and stock into the reserved marinade, then pour this over the meat mixture. Bring to the boil, stirring, then add the noodles to the pan and mix well until heated through. Serve at once.

SAUSAGE AND PEPPER STEW

GREECE

*This is a stove-top version of a dish more traditionally cooked
in individual clay bowls and baked in the oven. It's simple fare,
likely to be served at home or in the country taverns of Greece.*

SERVES 6–8

3 tbsp olive oil
700 g/1½ lb good quality
pork sausages, pricked
all over
2 onions, sliced into rings
5 peppers of various
colours, seeded and cut
into 1-cm/½-in strips
700 g/1½ lb tomatoes,
skinned and sliced into
rounds

3 garlic cloves, crushed
2 tsp dried oregano
125 ml/4 fl oz dry red
wine
salt and freshly ground
black pepper, to taste
chopped fresh sage, to
garnish

■ Heat the oil in a large frying pan and add the
sausages, turning them as they cook, until they are
evenly browned on all sides. Place the browned
sausages on absorbent kitchen paper to drain.
■ Add the onion to the frying pan with the peppers
and cook for about 10 minutes, or until softened. Stir in
the tomatoes, garlic and oregano. Return the sausages
to the pan and add the wine. Season with salt and
freshly ground black pepper and simmer, covered, for
about 1 hour, or until the sausages are cooked through,
adding a little extra water if necessary. Serve sprinkled
with chopped fresh sage.

SZECHUAN NOODLES

CHINA

SERVES 4

350 g/12 oz Chinese egg
  noodles
1 tbsp cornflour
2 tbsp dry sherry
4 tbsp chicken stock
4 tbsp light soy sauce
4 tbsp oil
2 green chillies, seeded
  and chopped
2 garlic cloves, crushed
5-cm/2-in piece fresh root
  ginger, peeled and cut
  into fine strips

225 g/8 oz lean boneless
  pork, cut into fine strips
1 red pepper, seeded and
  cut into fine, short strips
1 bunch spring onions, cut
  diagonally into fine
  slices
200-g/7-oz can bamboo
  shoots, drained and cut
  in strips
2.5-cm/1-in slice Chinese
  cabbage head,
  separated into pieces

■ Place the noodles in the pan and pour in enough boiling water to cover them. Bring back to the boil and cook for 2 minutes, then drain the noodles. While the noodles are cooking, blend the cornflour with the sherry, stock and soy sauce, then set aside.

■ Wipe the pan and heat the oil. Add the noodles, spreading them out thinly, and fry over medium to high heat until they are crisp and golden underneath, patting them down slightly into a thin cake – they will set more or less in shape. Use a large slice to turn the noodles over and brown the second side. Don't worry if the noodles break up slightly – the aim is to end up with some that are crisp and others that remain soft. Transfer the noodles to a large serving dish and keep hot.

■ Add the chillies, garlic, ginger and pork to the oil remaining in the pan. Stir-fry the mixture over high heat until the pork is browned. Add the pepper and spring onions and stir-fry for a further 2 minutes. Add the bamboo shoots and stir-fry for 1 minute.

■ Give the cornflour mixture a stir and pour it into the pan. Bring to the boil, stirring, and cook over high heat for 30 seconds. Mix in the Chinese cabbage and stir for less than a minute to heat through. Spoon the pork mixture over the noodles and serve at once.

PORK SPARE RIBS IN BARBECUE SAUCE

— UNITED KINGDOM —

SERVES 4

2 kg/4½ lb spare ribs

MARINADE
2 tbsp soy sauce
2 tbsp sherry
3 tbsp red wine vinegar
1 garlic clove, crushed
1 small onion, peeled and
   sliced
salt and freshly ground
   pepper
1 small piece root ginger,
   grated

BARBECUE SAUCE
2 garlic cloves, finely
   chopped
3 spring onions, washed
   and chopped
½ tsp fennel seeds
½ tsp cinnamon
½ tsp basil
2 cloves
2 tsp brown sugar
juice of ½ lemon
juice of ½ orange
2 tbsp red wine vinegar
300 ml/½ pt stock
2 tbsp soy sauce
425 g/15 oz canned
   peeled tomatoes
150 ml/¼ pt chicken stock

■ If possible, ask the butcher to trim the spare ribs to a good handling size, about 10 cm/4 in long.

■ Combine the marinade ingredients together and pour over the pork. Turn from time to time for about ½ to 1 hour, or even longer, if you wish. Deep fry the spare ribs for about 5 minutes and drain on kitchen paper.

■ Mix the ingredients for the sauce in a saucepan, wok or frying pan and bring to the boil. Add the spare ribs and simmer in the sauce for about 30 minutes. Add a little water and the remaining marinade to the pan to prevent it going dry.

VARIATION

Cook the marinated ribs on a wire rack over a roasting pan in a hot oven at 210°C/425°F/Gas Mark 7. Pour the sauce over the roasted meat.

PUERTO RICAN-STYLE ROAST PORK

—————— PUERTO RICO ——————

*Here's an enticing treatment of an economical cut:
leg of pork. This is a favourite dish in Puerto Rico, where it is known
as* Fabada Asturiana, *and the Puerto Rican love for assertive, spicy
flavours is amply demonstrated in this recipe. Adjust the amount of
onions and squash according to how many you wish to serve.*

SERVES 8–10

1 tbsp crushed garlic
3 tbsp olive oil
½ tsp dried oregano
  leaves, finely crumbled
¾ tsp ground cumin
1 tsp salt
½ tsp black pepper
4 large spring onions,
  chopped
50 g/2 oz fresh coriander,
  chopped
1 green pepper, chopped
225 ml/8 fl oz white rum
1 leg of pork (about 3 kg/
  7 lb with bone)
2 x 225-g/8-oz baking
  potatoes, scrubbed and
  cut lengthways into 8
  wedges

1–3 large red onions,
  each cut into 8
2–4 pieces squash, such
  as Hubbard or butternut
  or calabaza, peeled and
  cut into 2.5-cm/1-in
  slices (optional)
2–4 courgettes cut into
  2.5-cm/1-in slices
  (optional)

GRAVY

4 tbsp fat from drippings
  in roasting pan
25 g/1 oz plain flour
½ tsp black pepper
900 ml/1½ pt water or
  beef stock

■ Sauté the garlic in the olive oil until tender. In a blender or food processor, blend the olive oil-garlic mixture with the oregano, cumin, salt, pepper, spring onions, coriander, green pepper and rum to make a paste.

■ Place the meat in a non-reactive baking tin slightly larger than the meat. With a long, sharp knife, score the top of the roast in a diamond pattern, cutting through the rind and underlying fat almost to the meat. Rub the seasoning paste into the roast, then cover and marinate in the refrigerator overnight.

■ Heat the oven to 170°C/325°F/Gas Mark 3. Unwrap the meat and roast it for 2 hours. Add the potatoes, onions and squash, if using, to the roasting tin and brush with drippings. Roast for 1 hour, then add the courgettes, if using, and brush with drippings. Continue to roast for another 45 minutes (the meat should roast for a total of 32 to 35 minutes per 450 g/1 lb) or until a meat thermometer inserted in the thickest part (not touching the bone) registers 85°C/185°F and the vegetables are tender.

■ Remove the meat to a chopping board and cover loosely with foil (reserve the pan drippings for gravy). Leave to stand for 15 minutes before slicing. Arrange the vegetables on a dish and cover to keep warm.

■ If you are planning to reserve some of the meat and pan juices for other meals, proceed as follows: slice one-third of the pork and serve with the vegetables, reserving 225 ml/8 fl oz pan juices for gravy. Then slice half the remaining pork thinly (about 450 g/1 lb) and wrap tightly in heavy freezer bags. Shred the remaining meat (about 350 g/12 oz), cover and refrigerate. Sliced pork will keep for 2 weeks in the freezer; shredded about 1 week in the refrigerator.

■ To make the gravy, pour the fat into a medium saucepan and sprinkle the flour into it. Whisk over medium-high heat until smooth, scraping up browned bits. Gradually whisk in the water or beef stock until blended. Bring to a boil, reduce the heat and simmer for 5 minutes or until thickened, stirring 2 or 3 times.

SPAGHETTI WITH SMOKED SAUSAGE AND CARROTS

ITALY

SERVES 4

3 tbsp olive oil
1 onion, halved and thinly sliced
225 g/8 oz carrots, coarsely grated
450 g/1 lb smoked sausage, cut into strips

salt and freshly ground black pepper
450 g/1 lb spaghetti
50 g/2 oz butter

■ Heat the oil in a large frying pan. Add the onion and cook for 5 minutes, then add the carrots and sausage. Cook, stirring often, for about 10 minutes, until the pieces of sausage are browned in parts and the carrots are lightly cooked. Add seasoning to taste. Add the butter to the carrot and sausage mixture. Keep warm.
■ Cook the spaghetti in a large pan of boiling salted water. When *al dente*, drain, return to the pan and stir in the carrot and sausage mixture.

MEAT AND MUSHROOM PATTIES IN SAUCE

RUSSIA

This, together with ligzdinas – *meatballs stuffed with hard-boiled eggs – is Latvia's best-known main course. Neither is a subtle dish, but they appeal to hearty appetites gained from working in the open air.*

SERVES 6

2 tbsp vegetable oil
25 g/1 oz butter
2 onions, finely chopped
125 g/4 oz mushrooms
225 g/8 oz minced pork
225 g/8 oz minced veal
125 g/4 oz minced ham
3 tbsp finely chopped fresh parsley

¼ tsp dried thyme
salt and freshly ground black pepper
2 tbsp dry breadcrumbs
1 egg
175 ml/6 fl oz beef consommé or stock
150 ml/¼ pt sour cream

■ Melt half the oil and butter in a frying pan over medium heat. Add the onions and sauté gently for about 6 minutes, or until they are just softened. With a slotted spoon, remove half the onions and set aside. Add the mushrooms to the pan and continue cooking until they are very limp and most of the liquid has disappeared from the pan.
■ In a bowl, combine the three meats with the parsley, thyme and salt and pepper to taste, and the mushrooms and onions from the pan. Use your hands to mix thoroughly, then add the breadcrumbs and egg and continue to combine well. Shape the mixture into 6 patties and flatten them.
■ Add the remaining oil and butter to the pan. Melt over medium-high heat and sauté the patties until the meat is browned on both sides, about 15 minutes. Pour over consommé or stock, together with the reserved onions, and cook over high heat until the liquid is reduced by half. Reduce the heat to low and remove the patties to a serving dish; keep warm. Stir the sour cream into the sauce and pour over the patties. Serve immediately.

ROAST PORK WITH RHUBARB SAUCE

—— UNITED STATES ——

SERVES 4–6

900-g/2-lb boneless loin
  of pork
4 garlic cloves, peeled
  and cut into slivers
1 tsp salt
½ tsp freshly ground
  pepper
½ tsp mustard powder
½ tsp allspice
½ tsp cloves
½ tsp dried thyme leaves

RHUBARB SAUCE
700 g/1½ lb fresh
  rhubarb, diced
2 tbsp water
1 large green cooking
  apple, peeled, cored
  and diced
75 g/3 oz sugar
½ tsp grated orange peel
½ tsp allspice
⅛ tsp black pepper

■ Preheat the oven to 180°C/350°F/Gas Mark 4.
■ Trim the loin of all excess fat, leaving no more than 3-mm/⅛-in layer of fat. Cut deep, narrow slits all over the surface of the meat and insert slivers of garlic. Mix the spices, then rub all over the pork. Roll up the meat like a Swiss roll, and tie with string if it is not already tied.

Place the meat on a rack in a roasting tin. Roast for about 35 to 40 minutes per 450 g/1 lb until a thermometer inserted into the thickest part of the meat registers at least 60°C/140°F, and up to 77°C/170°F if you want the pork well done. Let the meat sit for about 15 minutes before carving it into slices 1 to 2.5 cm/½ to 1 in thick.
■ While the pork is roasting, make the sauce. Buy slim, crisp stalks of rhubarb. Trim off all leaves and roots. If the rhubarb seems tough and stringy, peel off the stringy parts. But try to avoid this by buying younger, tender stalks because the outer layer contains much of the colour and flavour.
■ Put all ingredients in a medium saucepan and simmer over low heat until apple is tender but not mushy, about 10 minutes. Taste and adjust the sugar if necessary; the sauce should not be too sweet, but neither should it be so tart that your lips pucker. Serve hot or cold with the pork.

ROAST PORK WITH
CHORIZO-RICE STUFFING

BRAZIL

SERVES 6

¼ tsp salt
2 tsp olive oil or butter
200 g/7 oz white rice
175–225 g/6–8 oz
  chorizo sausage
75 g/3 oz chopped onion

2 garlic cloves, crushed
40 g/1½ oz toasted pine
  nuts
1 kg/2¼ lb pork loin
325 g/11 oz salsa (see
  page 40)

■ Preheat the oven to 180°C/350°F/Gas Mark 4. Put 475 ml/16 fl oz water in a saucepan, add the salt and olive oil or butter and bring to the boil. Stir in the rice, cover and reduce the heat. Cook until the water has been absorbed and the rice is tender, 15 to 20 minutes.

■ Meanwhile, crumble the chorizo into a small frying pan. Cook over medium heat until the sausage is browned, 7 to 10 minutes, then remove with a slotted spoon and set aside. Discard all but 1 tablespoon of fat. Reheat the fat and add the onion. Sauté for 5 minutes, then add the garlic and pine nuts, and cook for 1 minute. Remove from the heat. Mix the chorizo and the onion mixture into the cooked rice

■ Unroll the pork loin, or make several lengthwise cuts so that it opens as much as possible into a thick, flat piece. Spoon some rice mixture into the centre of the loin, then reroll the meat and tie with string. You will have some rice left over. Put it in a lightly greased baking dish, cover and set aside.

■ Put the pork, cut side up, on a rack in a small roasting tin. Spread some of the salsa over the pork, coating it as much as possible, but make sure you have some salsa left over for basting. Put the pork in the oven and cook for approximately 1 hour, until the internal temperature measured with a meat thermometer reaches 71°C/160°F (although the meat is safe at 60°C/140°F). Baste the meat at least once with the additional salsa. During the last 5 minutes of cooking, put the leftover rice stuffing in the oven.

■ When the pork is done, remove it from the oven and let stand for 15 minutes before carving it into slices. Let the stuffing continue to cook while the pork rests.

MEAT AND **R**ICE **B**ALLS IN **L**EMON **S**AUCE

GREECE

Known as yuverlakia *(little spheres) in Greek, this dish is a cross between a hearty soup and stew.*

SERVES 8–10

450 g/1 lb minced pork
150 g/5 oz long-grain
   rice
1 large onion, finely
   chopped
2 garlic cloves, crushed
4 tbsp very finely chopped
   fresh parsley
2 tbsp chopped fresh mint
1 tsp dried oregano

1 egg yolk
salt and freshly ground
   black pepper, to taste
flour, for dredging
3 tbsp olive oil
3 eggs, beaten
freshly squeezed juice of
   2 lemons, strained
chopped fresh parsley, to
   garnish

■ Combine the pork, rice, onion, garlic and herbs in a large mixing bowl. Add the egg yolk and season with salt and pepper. Mix thoroughly to combine all the ingredients. Using slightly damp hands, shape the mixture into 5-cm/2-in balls and dredge with flour.

■ Place the olive oil in a large, deep frying pan with the meatballs. Add enough boiling water to just cover the meatballs. Cover and simmer for 35 to 40 minutes, or until the meat and rice are cooked, adding a little extra water to keep the meatballs covered during cooking if necessary.

■ To make the lemon sauce; beat together the eggs and lemon juice until frothy. Whisk in 2 tablespoons of the cooking liquid from the meatballs, whisking vigorously to prevent curdling. Remove the frying pan from the heat and pour the egg mixture over the meatballs. Return the frying pan to the heat and stir continuously, until thickened. Do not allow the sauce to boil. Transfer the meatballs and sauce to a warm serving dish and garnish with chopped fresh parsley.

CURRIED PORK CHOPS WITH RICE PILAF

BARBADOS

This is a subtly seasoned Creole dish that complements the curried rice. Add a tossed salad for a meal that can be put together in less than half an hour.

SERVES 4

200 g/7 oz long-grain white rice
2 tbsp vegetable oil
175 g/6 oz raisins
½ tsp ground cumin
½ tsp salt
½ tsp freshly ground black pepper

300 ml/10 fl oz chicken stock
50 ml/2 fl oz water
1½ tsp curry powder
⅛ tsp ground cinnamon
⅛ tsp chilli powder
8 very thin pork chops (900 g/2 lb in total)

■ Toast the rice in 1 tablespoon oil in a saucepan for 2 to 3 minutes until golden. Stir in the raisins, ¼ teaspoon cumin, salt and pepper. Cook for 1 minute. Add the stock and water. Simmer, covered, until the liquids are absorbed by the rice, about 15 to 20 minutes.
■ Meanwhile, combine the curry powder, remaining cumin, cinnamon and chilli powder. Rub on the chops.
■ Divide the remaining oil between two frying pans and heat to moderately hot. Divide the chops between the frying pans and cook, covered, for 3 minutes on each side until cooked through. Alternatively, cook in two stages in one frying pan, keeping the first batch of chops warm. Serve with the rice.

NORTHERN PORK CURRY

THAILAND

This dish originally comes from across the Burmese border, as shown by the use of tamarind and turmeric. The palm sugar adds an intentional slight sweetness.

SERVES 6

4 stalks lemon grass, chopped
1 tbsp chopped galangal
1 tbsp shrimp paste
4 dried red chillies, chopped
1 kg/2¼ lb pork belly, cut into small 1-cm/½-in thick strips
750 ml/1¼ pt cold water
1 tbsp turmeric
1 tsp black soy sauce

10 shallots, sliced
40 g/1½ oz palm sugar
40 g/1½ oz chopped and pounded ginger
50 ml/2 fl oz tamarind juice
2 tbsp chopped garlic
½ tbsp marinated soya beans
fish sauce, to taste (optional)

■ Pound the lemon grass, galangal, shrimp paste and chillies with a mortar and pestle or in a blender until fine, then mix with the pork. Put in a pan with the water, turmeric and soy sauce. Bring to a boil and cook until tender, about 15 minutes, then add the rest of the ingredients. Boil again for 5 to 8 minutes and remove from the heat. Taste and season with fish sauce, if necessary.

CABBAGE WITH **K**ABANOS

POLAND

A small amount of diced smoked pork or smoked bacon may be used in place of kabanos. Serve with Polish rye bread.

SERVES 4

1 large onion, thinly sliced
25 g/1 oz fat
225 g/8 oz kabanos, sliced
700 g/1½ lb green cabbage, trimmed of tough stalks and shredded

300 ml/½ pt water
salt and freshly ground black pepper
1 tbsp plain flour
4 tbsp soured cream

■ In a heavy-based flameproof casserole, cook the onion in the fat for about 15 minutes, until soft but not browned. Add the kabanos, stir well and cook for 2 minutes. Stir in the cabbage, then pour in the water and add a little seasoning. Bring to the boil, cover and cook, just boiling, for 5 minutes.
■ Combine the flour with the soured cream to make a smooth paste, and stir into the cabbage. Simmer, stirring all the time, for a further 3 to 5 minutes, until thick.

PORK **C**ASSEROLE WITH **C**UMIN

PORTUGAL

SERVES 4

700 g/1½ lb boneless lean pork, cut into 3.75-cm/1½-in pieces
1½ tsp ground cumin
3 garlic cloves, crushed
1 bay leaf
salt and pepper

75 ml/3 fl oz dry white wine
2 tsp lemon juice
2 tbsp olive oil
1 onion, finely chopped
10–12 stoned black olives
lemon wedges, to serve

■ Put the pork into a mixing bowl and add the cumin, garlic, bay leaf and seasoning. Pour over the wine and lemon juice. Stir to mix, then cover and leave in the refrigerator for 6 to 8 hours, stirring a few times.
■ Preheat oven to 170°C/325°F/Gas Mark 3. Drain the pork, reserving the marinade. Heat the oil in a heavy-based flameproof casserole, add the onion and cook until softened. Add the pork and fry until browned, stirring occasionally. Stir in the reserved marinade, cover and cook in the oven for 1 to 1½ hours until the pork is tender. Scatter over the olives and serve with lemon wedges.

ROAST PORK CALYPSO

—— JAMAICA ——

SERVES 6

1.75-kg/4-lb piece of pork
475 ml/16 fl oz cold
  water
1 tbsp vinegar
1 tbsp salt
3 garlic cloves, crushed

1 tsp thyme
1 onion, grated
1 tsp ground cloves
1 tbsp chopped fresh
  parsley

■ Place the pork in a large saucepan, cover with the cold water and add the vinegar, salt, garlic and thyme. Leave to marinate for several hours.

■ Meanwhile, mix the onion, cloves and parsley in a bowl. Preheat the oven to 160°C/325°F/Gas Mark 3.

■ When the pork is ready, remove it from the saucepan and make 5-cm/2-in long gashes all over. Fill the holes with the onion mixture. Pour the marinade into a baking dish. Lay the pork in the dish and roast in the preheated oven for 30 minutes, or until it is done.

STEAMED MINCED PORK WITH SALTFISH

VIETNAM

SERVES 4

50 g/2 oz saltfish
1 tbsp Nuoc Mam sauce or light soy sauce
1 tsp sugar
450 g/1 lb lean pork, minced
1 tbsp finely chopped spring onions (white part only)
1 tbsp dark soy sauce
2 tsp rice wine or dry sherry
½ tsp sugar
salt and freshly ground black pepper
2 tbsp sesame oil
1 egg, well beaten
1 tbsp cornflour
2 level tbsp plain flour

■ Soak the saltfish overnight, taking care to change the water at least once. Strip off the dark skin and discard. Shred the saltfish, rinse and squeeze dry. Chop it roughly and put it in a mixing bowl with the Nuoc Mam sauce and sugar, stir and then set aside.

■ Chop the minced pork until it is smooth. Scoop into a mixing bowl and add the spring onions, soy sauce, rice wine, sugar, salt, black pepper and 1 tablespoon sesame oil. Blend thoroughly. Add the beaten egg, a little at a time, mixing all the while. Sprinkle in the cornflour and plain flour, stirring them into the mixture until absolutely smooth. Divide into 16 portions.

■ Squeeze the saltfish to remove excess moisture. Add 1 tablespoon sesame oil and mix thoroughly. Divide the mixture into 16 portions.

■ Grease your palms with oil and place one portion of meat in the palm of one hand. Flatten with the fingers of the other hand. Put a portion of saltfish in the centre and fold the meat over it. Roll lightly into a ball. Make a total of 16 balls.

■ Steam the balls over a high heat for at least 15 minutes and transfer them to a serving dish with the meat juices.

TOLOSA RED BEAN STEW WITH PORK

SPAIN

Tolosa is famous for its kidney beans, which are long and as black as coal. Ninety years ago, however, they were red. Basques have always adored red beans and still do, so in this recipe they are red! The traditional dish contains the red chorizo *sausage and the black* morcilla, *along with cured pork. It can work equally well as a starter.*

SERVES 4

450 g/1 lb red beans, soaked overnight
150 g/5 oz pork belly or boiling bacon, in one piece
1 large onion, finely chopped
2 tbsp olive oil
2 tbsp chopped ham fat or more olive oil
2 chorizo sausages
1 morcillo or 150 g/5 oz black pudding, preferably made with onion
1 large green pepper, seeded and chopped
salt and freshly ground black pepper
2 garlic cloves, finely chopped

■ Drain the beans and put them in a pan with the salt pork and half the chopped onion. Add 1 tablespoon of oil and cover with at least 2.5 cm/1 in of water. Bring to a good rolling boil then turn down the heat, cover and simmer gently for 2 hours or until the meat is almost tender. Watch that the water level remains high enough, adding more if necessary, but always in small quantities.

■ Fry the ham to give off grease, or heat the oil in a pan. Slice and fry the chorizos and morcilla or black pudding (removing any plastic skin) with the chopped pepper.

■ Remove the cured pork or bacon from the beans and chop it into cubes. Check the amount of liquid in the beans: it should now be well reduced (if not, then pour some off). Add all the meats to the pot and season everything well.

■ Fry the remaining onion in same pan you used for the sausage, adding the garlic at the end. Stir into the beans and simmer 10 minutes more.

GINGERY PORK CHOPS WITH CURRIED MANGO

JAMAICA

*No plain-Jane pork chops these! This spicy-fruity main dish is best
served with simpler side dishes, such as plain white rice or black bean dishes.
A spinach salad would add some contrasting colour and texture.*

SERVES 6

6 pork loin chops, about
2.5 cm/1 in thick,
trimmed of fat
1½ tsp grated root ginger
or ground ginger
3 garlic cloves, crushed
125 ml/4 fl oz dry sherry
or dry wine
175 g/6 oz ginger or
orange marmalade
50 ml/2 fl oz soy sauce
2 tbsp light sesame oil

CURRIED MANGO
2 mangoes, cut in bite-size
chunks (or canned
unsweetened mango or
4 nectarines)
25 g/1 oz butter or
margarine, melted
50 g/2 oz demerara
sugar
1–1½ tsp curry powder

■ Make the Curried Mango first. Preheat the oven to
180°C/350°F/Gas Mark 4. Place the drained mango in a
pie dish. Combine the butter or margarine, sugar and
curry powder and spoon over the fruit. Bake in the
oven for 30 minutes. Keep warm until the pork chops
are done.

■ With a knife point, make 6 incisions less than
8 mm/¼ in deep, on each side of the chops. Make a
paste of the ginger and garlic and rub it into the meat
on both sides, spreading any remaining paste on top of
the chops. Set aside.

■ Combine the sherry or wine, marmalade, soy sauce
and sesame oil. Mix well and pour over the chops.
Cook uncovered in the oven for about 15 minutes,
basting and turning occasionally.

LAMB

SPICY MINCE WITH PEAS

— INDIA —

Serve this quick mince dish and its cucumber raita topping with fragrant pilau rice or hot naan bread.

SERVES 4

450 g/1 lb minced lamb
2 tbsp ground coriander
1 tsp ground ginger
6 green cardamoms
2 bay leaves
juice of 1 lemon
salt and freshly ground
    black pepper
2 tbsp oil
1 onion, chopped
2 garlic cloves, crushed
1 cinnamon stick
1 tbsp cumin seeds

1 tbsp mustard seeds
1 large potato, diced
125 g/4 oz frozen peas
50 g/2 oz raisins

TOPPING
¼ cucumber, peeled and
    diced
125 ml/4 fl oz natural
    yoghurt
1 tbsp chopped fresh mint
mint sprigs to garnish
    (optional)

■ Place the lamb in a basin with the coriander, ginger, cardamoms, bay leaves and lemon juice. Add seasoning and mix thoroughly. If possible, cover and leave to marinate for several hours or even overnight in the refrigerator.

■ Heat the oil, then stir-fry the onion, garlic, cinnamon, cumin, mustard and potato until the potato dice are browned all over. Make sure that the pan does not overheat or the spices will burn. Add the mince mixture and continue to stir-fry until the meat is browned. Stir in the peas and raisins, and then cook for a further 5 minutes. Taste for seasoning, then transfer to a heated serving dish.

■ For the topping, mix the cucumber and yoghurt with the chopped mint, then swirl this through the spicy mince. Garnish the dish with fresh mint, if wished, and serve at once.

CHUNKS OF LAMB IN FILO PASTRY

— GREECE —

This dish would be perfect for a meze picnic. Easily made in advance, it can also be frozen unbaked, then thawed and finished off in the oven when required.

SERVES 10–15

3.6-kg/8-lb leg of lamb
4 garlic cloves, cut into
    slivers
salt and freshly ground
    black pepper, to taste
2 tsp dried oregano
350 g/12 oz butter,
    melted
3 tbsp freshly squeezed
    lemon juice

2 carrots, peeled
2 celery sticks, trimmed
1 onion, quartered
450 g/1 lb filo pastry,
    thawed if frozen
450 g/1 lb fresh white
    breadcrumbs
225/8 oz feta cheese,
    crumbled

■ Preheat the oven to 190°C/375°F/Gas Mark 5. Using a sharp knife, make small incisions all over the lamb and insert the slivers of garlic into them. Place the lamb in a roasting tin. Season with salt and freshly ground black pepper and sprinkle with the oregano. Drizzle over a little of the melted butter and pour over the lemon juice. Add the carrot, celery and onion to the pan and roast the lamb for 2 to 2½ hours, until the meat is tender and the juices run clear. Transfer the joint to a chopping board and cut the meat into 2.5-cm/1-in chunks, discarding the fat and bone. Allow the meat to cool.

■ Take one sheet of filo pastry, keeping the remainder covered with a slightly damp cloth, and brush lightly with melted butter. Fold the sheet in half. Brush once again with melted butter, then sprinkle over a few of the breadcrumbs.

■ Place a few chunks of meat towards one end of the pastry and sprinkle with a little of the cheese. Fold up the pastry around the filling, enclosing it securely, and place seam-side down on a lightly oiled baking sheet. Repeat with the remaining filo pastry and filling. Brush the parcels with the remaining melted butter and bake for about 30 minutes, or until the pastry has turned crisp and golden.

LAMB AND SALT BEEF STEW

BARBADOS

SERVES 6

225 g/8 oz lean salt beef
50 g/2 oz butter or margarine
1 tbsp vegetable oil
900 g/2 lb boned lamb or goat cut into 2.5-cm/1-in pieces
225 g/8 oz onions, finely chopped
1 large tomato, skinned and chopped
2 tsp peeled and chopped fresh root ginger

25 g/1 oz green pepper, chopped
1 fat garlic clove, chopped
½ fresh hot pepper, chopped
1 tsp salt
2 tsp ground cumin
2 tbsp lime or lemon juice
600 ml/1 pt water
3 potatoes, peeled and diced
2 cucumbers, peeled and diced

■ Put the salt beef in a saucepan, cover with cold water, bring to the boil and boil for 30 minutes. Drain the meat and cut it into cubes.

■ Heat the butter or margarine and oil in a large saucepan, then add the lamb or goat and brown it all over. Remove the meat and set to one side.

■ Add the onions to the saucepan and cook for 5 minutes. Then add the tomato, ginger, green pepper, garlic, hot pepper, salt and cumin. Cook for 10 minutes, stirring all the time.

■ Stir in the prepared salt beef, lamb, lime or lemon juice and water. Cook for 1 hour over low heat. Add the potatoes and cucumber and simmer for 20 more minutes.

S**PICED** L**AMB** C**HOPS**

LEBANON

S**ERVES** 6

125 g/4 oz butter	mint
½ tsp Lebanese spice mix	1 tbsp freshly chopped flat-
(see page 11)	leaved parsley
1¼ tsp ground cardamom	1 garlic clove, crushed
¾ tsp ground ginger	12 trimmed loin lamb
¼ tsp ground nutmeg	chops
large pinch of coriander	salt and freshly ground
pinch of cloves	pepper
1 tbsp freshly chopped	

■ In a small saucepan, slowly melt the butter over low heat. Add all the spices, the mint and the parsley, stir once or twice, then remove from the heat. Stir in the garlic and leave for at least 1 hour at room temperature to allow all the flavours to mingle.

■ Season the lamb chops with salt and pepper to taste. Melt the seasoned butter, if it has congealed, and brush the meat with it. Cook the chops over grey-ashed coals or under a preheated grill for about 6 to 8 minutes a side, until the outside is well browned but the inside is still pink. Transfer the chops to serving plates and pour over the remaining seasoned butter.

S**TUFFED** P**EPPERS**

RUSSIA

This is a Westernized version of the stuffed peppers one would encounter in Russia. Some of the dried fruits which give it distinction are not to be found here, but this recipe is still redolent of the Silk Road and the East.

S**ERVES** 6

6 medium, well-shaped red	2 eggs, beaten
peppers	1 tsp ground allspice
1 tbsp vegetable oil	½ tsp ground cumin
700 g/1½ lb minced lean	½ tsp ground cinnamon
lamb	large pinch of cayenne
2 small onions, chopped	pepper
225 g/8 oz cooked long-	salt and freshly ground
grain white rice	black pepper
3 tbsp sultanas	225 ml/8 fl oz Greek
3 tbsp tomato purée	yoghurt
2 tbsp honey	

■ Cut the tops from the peppers and carefully remove the ribs and seeds from the insides. Rinse and drain the shells.

■ Heat the oil in a large frying pan and add the lamb. Cook over medium heat, breaking up the lamb with a wooden spoon, until the meat is browned. Stir in the onions and cook until they are soft and lightly coloured. Remove the pan from the heat and drain off the fat.

■ Stir in the rice and sultanas; cook for 2 minutes. Add the tomato purée, honey, eggs and spices; season to taste and combine well.

■ Preheat the oven to 190°C/375°F/Gas Mark 5. Divide the filling equally between the 6 peppers, pressing it down tightly, then pack them into a shallow casserole. Bake for about 40 minutes, until the tops are browned and the peppers are soft. Serve hot or cold, with a bowl of yoghurt to spoon over.

MEATBALLS IN TOMATO SAUCE

GREECE

This rich, tasty dish can be made well in advance and kept in the fridge – in fact, it tastes better reheated the next day.

SERVES 6–8

700 g/1½ lb minced lamb
2 slices brown bread, crusts removed
4 tbsp milk
1 tbsp olive oil
1 onion, chopped
1 tomato, skinned, seeded and chopped
125 g/4 oz long-grain rice
1 tbsp chopped fresh mint
pinch of ground cinnamon

2 tbsp chopped fresh parsley
1 egg, beaten
50 ml/2 fl oz red wine
salt and freshly ground black pepper, to taste
1.2 ltr/2 pt water
4 tbsp tomato purée
1 garlic clove, crushed
chopped fresh parsley, to garnish

■ Place the minced lamb in a large mixing bowl. Place the bread on a plate, sprinkle with the milk and allow to soak for 10 minutes, or until all the milk has been absorbed. Add the bread to the mixing bowl. Using your hand, mix the meat and bread together.

■ Heat the olive oil in a small saucepan and sauté the onion and chopped tomato flesh for about 5 minutes. Add to the mixing bowl with the rice, mint, cinnamon, parsley, beaten egg, wine, salt and freshly ground black pepper. Mix well to combine all the ingredients.

■ Place the water in a large, deep frying pan and stir in the tomato purée. Add the garlic and heat gently to bring to the boil. Simmer for 5 minutes.

■ Using slightly damp hands, shape the meat mixture into round balls, about the size of a golf ball, and carefully place them in the simmering tomato sauce. Cover the frying pan and cook for about 30 minutes, or until the rice is cooked and the sauce has thickened.

FRIED LAMB WITH LEMON JUICE

SPAIN

SERVES 4

800 g/1¾ lb trimmed
   tender lamb, in strips
salt and freshly ground
   black pepper
2 tbsp olive oil
1 onion, chopped
2 garlic cloves, finely
   chopped

2 tsp paprika
250 ml/9 fl oz stock or
   water
juice of 1 lemon
2 tbsp finely chopped
   parsley

■ Season the lamb with salt and pepper. Heat the oil in a casserole over your hottest burner and add the meat in handfuls. Add the onion, too, and keep turning the meat around with a wooden spoon. Add more meat as each batch is sealed, then the garlic and more oil if necessary.

■ When the meat is golden and the onion soft, sprinkle with paprika and add the stock or water. Continue cooking over a medium heat until the liquid has virtually gone.

■ Sprinkle with the lemon juice and parsley, cover and simmer for 5 minutes. Check the seasonings before serving.

LAMB KNUCKLE STEW

LEBANON

Lamb knuckle is familiar to Western foodies as the main ingredient of that Greek taverna staple lamb kleftiko. It is an economical dish in any guise; in Lebanon it is often stewed with green beans, or as here, with chick-peas.

SERVES 4

1 tbsp olive oil
2 onions, sliced
3 garlic cloves, finely
   chopped
1 tsp allspice
2 tsp ground cumin
pinch crushed dried red
   pepper flakes
1 bay leaf, crushed
4 meaty knuckles of lamb
   (about 350 g/12 oz
   each)

2 x 400-g/14-oz cans
   chick-peas, drained and
   rinsed
2 x 400-g/14-oz cans
   chopped tomatoes
475 ml/16 fl oz lamb or
   beef stock
salt and freshly ground
   pepper
1 lemon
50 g/2 oz chopped
   coriander

■ Preheat the oven to 220°C/475°F/Gas Mark 7. Pour the oil into a casserole in which the knuckles will fit in one layer with space to spare. Heat over medium heat, add the onion and sauté for 4 minutes, then add the garlic and continue cooking until both onion and garlic are limp and lightly coloured, about 6 minutes.

■ Remove the hot onions with a slotted spoon to a large bowl, stir in the spices and bay leaf, and reserve. Add the knuckles to the casserole, turning in the oil to brown them. Transfer the casseroled lamb to the oven, and bake for 35 minutes, turning the knuckles occasionally.

■ Add the chick-peas, tomatoes and stock to the onions in the bowl and mix together. Remove the casserole from the oven, pour the chick-pea and tomato mixture over the knuckles and season to taste. Bring the stew to the boil on top of the stove, then cover and continue baking for another hour on the lowest shelf of the oven. Test the knuckle with a knife for doneness; it should pierce easily.

■ Squeeze the juice from the lemon and sprinkle it and the coriander over the stew. Serve immediately.

LAMB, BEANSPROUT AND BEAN SALAD

VIETNAM

SERVES 4

125 g/4 oz crispy roast
  leg of lamb, thinly sliced
  and cut into 1 x 2.5-cm/
  ½ x 1-in strips
125 g/4 oz beansprouts
125 g/4 oz French beans,
  blanched
125 g/4 oz broccoli
  florets, blanched
6 lettuce leaves
3 large tomatoes, cut into
  wedges
1 large cucumber, peeled
  and sliced
½ medium green pepper,
  cut in strips
2 medium-sized onions,
  finely sliced into rings
6 spring onion curls
3 hard-boiled eggs, halved

DRESSING
75 g/3 oz unsalted
  roasted peanuts
125 ml/4 fl oz lemon juice
3 tbsp vinegar
4 garlic cloves
3 tbsp fresh coriander,
  chopped
40 g/1½ oz Nuoc Mam
  sauce or Maggi liquid
  seasoning

GARNISH
1 hard-boiled egg, sliced
fresh coriander, chopped

■ Blend all the dressing ingredients in a blender and set aside. Arrange the salad ingredients on a large dish and pour dressing over the top.

CURRIED LAMB WITH LENTILS

SURINAM

This Indo-Caribbean dish can also be made with goat meat

SERVES 6

2 tbsp oil
1 tbsp cumin seeds
1 tsp ground turmeric
1 large onion, chopped
2 garlic cloves, crushed
5 cm/2 in root ginger,
  peeled and finely
  chopped
900 g/2 lb boned lamb or
  goat meat, cubed

1 hot pepper, chopped
225 g/8 oz lentils,
  washed and drained
400-g/14-oz can
  tomatoes, drained and
  chopped
1 tsp salt
freshly ground black
  pepper
600 ml/1 pt cold water

■ Heat the oil in a flameproof casserole, then add the cumin, turmeric, onion, garlic and ginger. Fry them for 5 minutes over a medium heat. Add the lamb, or goat meat and cook for 5 more minutes.

■ Stir in the hot pepper, lentils, tomatoes and seasoning to taste. Add the cold water, bring to the boil, then lower the heat, cover and simmer for 1 hour until the meat is tender and the sauce has become thick. Serve with naan bread or steamed rice and mango chutney.

SPICY LAMB STEW WITH MINT AND SAGE

———— GREECE ————

SERVES 6–8

50 ml/2 fl oz olive oil
900 g/2 lb lean lamb
    fillet, cut into 2.5-cm/
    1-in cubes
1 onion, chopped
2 carrots, diced
125 ml/4 fl oz dry white
    wine
salt and freshly ground
    black pepper, to taste

125 g/4 oz flaked
    almonds
900 ml/1½ pt water
225 g/8 oz long-grain
    rice
50 g/2 oz sultanas
50 g/2 oz raisins
½ tsp dried sage
1 tsp dried mint

■ Heat the oil in a large saucepan. Add the cubed meat and cook, turning frequently, until evenly browned. Add the onion and carrots and cook for about 5 minutes. Stir in the wine and season with salt and freshly ground black pepper. Bring to the boil, then cover and cook for 10 minutes.

■ Meanwhile, toast the almonds, either under the grill or in a heavy-based frying pan, until they are golden. Set aside.

■ Stir the water into the meat mixture and continue to simmer for a further 30 minutes, stirring occasionally. Add the rice, sultanas, raisins, sage and mint to the stew and adjust the seasoning, if necessary. Simmer, covered, for a further 30 to 35 minutes, or until the rice is cooked and the meat is tender, adding a little extra water during cooking if necessary. Scatter the toasted almonds over the stew and serve hot.

LAMB IN A HOT GARLIC SAUCE

VIETNAM

SERVES 4

225 g/8 oz fresh spinach
  or any green vegetable
2 tbsp vegetable oil
225 g/8 oz lean lamb,
  thinly sliced
4 garlic cloves, finely
  chopped
freshly ground white
  pepper

½ tsp sugar
1 tbsp Nuoc Mam sauce
  or 1 tbsp light soy sauce
  and 1 tsp anchovy
  essence
1 tbsp oyster sauce
fresh sprigs of mint and/or
  coriander to garnish

■ Blanch the greens in boiling water for 1 minute. Drain and place on a serving dish.
■ Heat the oil in a wok and stir-fry the lamb until nearly cooked. This should not take more than 2 minutes. Add the garlic, pepper, sugar, Nuoc Mam sauce and oyster sauce and stir-fry until the lamb is completely cooked and tender.
■ Pour the lamb and sauce over the greens. Garnish with mint and/or coriander sprigs.

LAMB CHOPS WITH CHEESE

GREECE

An unusual but delicious combination of lamb and cheese, cooked in packets of aluminium foil to retain all the natural flavours.

SERVES 4

4 lamb chump chops
25 g/1 oz butter
1 onion, sliced
2 garlic cloves, crushed
3 tomatoes, sliced
3 tsp dried oregano

salt and freshly ground
  black pepper, to taste
125 g/4 oz kaseri or
  Gruyère cheese, sliced
  thinly

■ Fry the chops, with no extra fat, in a frying pan for about 3 minutes on each side, or until evenly browned. Cut out four 30-cm/12-in squares of kitchen foil and place a chop in the centre of each square.
■ Preheat the oven to 180°C/350°F/Gas Mark 4. Melt the butter in the frying pan and sauté the onion and garlic for about 3 minutes. Using a spoon, place some onion mixture on each chop. Divide the slices of tomato between the chops, placing them on top of the onion mixture. Sprinkle each serving with oregano and season with salt and freshly ground black pepper. Sprinkle the cheese evenly over the four chops.
■ Gather up the sides of each piece of foil and pinch them together in the middle to completely encase the chops. Place the packets on a baking sheet in the oven for 1½ to 2 hours, or until the meat is tender and cooked through. Serve in the foil packets.

MEAT AND TOMATO STEW

RUSSIA

*This traditional dish is made as frequently with chicken as it is with lamb.
In the old manner it is cooked in a large iron pot over hot coals,
but this version has been adapted to suit the modern hob.*

SERVES 6

1 tbsp vegetable or olive oil
900 g/2 lb lamb steaks, trimmed of fat and cubed
2 onions, chopped
700 g/1½ lb whole Roma or plum tomatoes, skinned, seeded and roughly chopped
3 large potatoes, peeled and roughly cubed
salt and freshly ground black pepper
50 g/2 oz fresh coriander, chopped
50 g/2 oz fresh, flat-leaved parsley, chopped
5 fresh basil leaves, chopped
8 garlic cloves, crushed

■ Heat the oil in a large enamelled or stainless steel casserole until very hot but not smoking. Tilt to cover the bottom with the oil. Add the lamb pieces and brown, stirring with a wooden spoon, for 10 minutes.

■ When the meat is coloured, add the onions and continue to stir until they are soft. Add the tomatoes and use the spoon to crush them. Stir in the potatoes and seasoning to taste. Cover and simmer over low heat for about 45 minutes, or until the meat and potatoes are tender and the tomatoes have become a mushy sauce.

■ Uncover and turn up the heat. Stir in the herbs and garlic and continue to stir as the sauce bubbles for 10 minutes. Take off the heat, cover and leave to stand for 5 to 8 minutes before serving.

LAMB AND PASTA HOTPOT

ITALY

*This is a heart-warming winter stew! Beef, pork or bacon may all be used
instead of lamb. Offer some crusty bread to mop up the juices*

SERVES 4

1 tbsp oil
575 g/1¼ lb lean
  boneless lamb, cubed
1 onion, chopped
2 carrots, diced
2 rosemary sprigs
salt and freshly ground
  black pepper

600 ml/1 pt light ale
600 ml/1 pt water
225 g/8 oz frozen peas
450 g/1 lb pasta spirals
150 ml/¼ pt soured cream
paprika
croûtons, to serve

COOK'S TIP

*Make croûtons by frying small cubes or triangles of
bread in a mixture of olive oil and butter until golden.
Drain on kitchen paper.*

■ Heat the oil in a large, flameproof casserole or
heavy-based saucepan. Add the lamb and brown the
cubes all over. Stir in the onion, carrots, rosemary sprigs
and seasoning. Cook stirring, for a few minutes, then
add the ale and water. Bring just to the boil, reduce the
heat and cover the pan. Leave the hotpot to simmer for
1¼ hours, stirring occasionally until the lamb is tender
and the cooking liquor is well flavoured.

■ Taste for seasoning, then add the peas. Bring back to
the boil, reduce the heat and cover the pot. Simmer for
15 minutes. Add the pasta, stir well, then bring back to
the boil. Partially cover the pan and cook for 5 minutes,
allowing the hotpot to only just boil.

■ Top individual portions of the hotpot with soured
cream and a dusting of paprika. Sprinkle with croûtons
and serve piping hot.

FRIED LAMB WITH PAPRIKA AND VINEGAR

—— SPAIN ——

Yearling lamb is fried and seasoned with the local paprika, the most aromatic and tasty in Spain, or with guindilla, *which is Spain's hot chilli. With it goes the cloudy local* cañamero, *which looks like beer, but tastes like dry sherry. Either of these makes a good accompanying drink.*

SERVES 4

1 slice stale bread
3 tbsp red wine vinegar
2–4 tbsp olive oil
800 g/1¾ lb tender, lean lamb shoulder, diced
salt and freshly ground black pepper
6 garlic cloves

1 guindilla, or ½ dried chilli, seeded and chopped, or a pinch of cayenne pepper
6 cloves
4 tbsp chopped fresh parsley
1 tbsp paprika, preferably from Jarandilla

■ Sprinkle the bread with vinegar. Fry it in a casserole in 2 tablespoons of hot oil and reserve. Season the lamb with black pepper and salt. Put the casserole over your hottest burner and add the meat in handfuls, with 3 finely chopped garlic cloves and the guindilla, chilli, or cayenne pepper, turning it and keeping it moving with a wooden spoon. Add more lamb as each batch is sealed, with more oil as necessary.

■ Crush 3 garlic cloves in a mortar (or an electric herb mill). Crush in the cloves and parsley, reducing everything to a paste.

■ Sprinkle the lamb with paprika, stirring in the paste and 200 ml/7 fl oz of water. Cook, covered, until the lamb is tender (about 30 minutes) and the liquid reduced to a few spoonfuls. Finally, purée the reserved bread and stir in to thicken the sauce. Check the seasonings before serving.

LAMB TIKKA

—— INDIA ——

SERVES 4

575 g/1¼ lb leg of lamb, cut in a thick slice
150 ml/¼ pt natural yoghurt
1 tsp chilli powder
1 tsp crushed coriander
1 tsp garam masala
½ tsp salt
juice of 1 fresh lime or lemon

GARNISH
8 lettuce leaves
2 tomatoes, sliced
12 slices of cucumber
1 small onion, peeled and finely sliced
1 lemon or lime, quartered

■ Leg of lamb sliced about 1.5 cm/½ in thick is best for this dish. Remove any bone or gristle. Cut into 1.5-cm/½-in thick cubes.

■ Mix yoghurt with all other ingredients in a plastic bag or a flat dish. Add the meat to the marinate and allow to soak for several hours. Turn from time to time. Divide the meat on to 4 skewers and cook under a hot grill, turning every 2 minutes.

■ Serve each portion off the skewer with rice and a green salad. Garnish with the above ingredients.

SPICY LAMB WITH PEPPERS

SPAIN

Lamb from Navarre is famous and so is this dish. Old recipes use dried, pounded choricero *peppers, but nowadays fresh peppers are used. It needs neither wine nor water to produce a succulent red purée that coats the meat perfectly.*

SERVES 4–6

1.5 kg/3 lb shoulder of lamb, cubed
2–4 tbsp olive oil
salt and freshly ground black pepper
2 onions, chopped
2 garlic cloves, finely chopped
4–6 big ripe tomatoes, skinned and seeded

2 big baked red peppers, skinned and seeded, or canned pimentos
2 tbsp finely chopped parsley
1 bay leaf
good pinch of cayenne pepper

■ Trim and season the lamb. Heat 3 tablespoons of oil in a casserole then fry the lamb in 2 batches over a high heat until browned on all sides; remove from the pot and set aside.
■ Fry the onions, with more oil if needed, adding the garlic at the end. Chop the tomato and peppers or pimentos finely (or process), then add them to the pot with the parsley, bay leaf and cayenne pepper. Cook for a few minutes to make a sauce, then season and return the lamb.
■ Simmer for 1 hour, covered, over a very low heat. It makes its own liquid, but check occasionally that the heat is low enough so it does not dry. Taste for seasoning, paying particular attention to the balance of pepper and cayenne pepper – the dish should be spicy. Surprisingly, you may even have to boil off excess liquid.

ORIENTAL GINGER LAMB

CHINA

This is a dish to make when you can buy juicy, young ginger, which is plump and thin-skinned – look out for it in Chinese supermarkets. Remember to warn unsuspecting guests that there are whole ginger slices in among the pieces of meat – when the ginger is young and tender, the slices are, of course, perfectly edible, but many people prefer to avoid them.

SERVES 4

450 g/1 lb lean boneless lamb, cut into small, thin slices
5-cm/2-in piece young fresh root ginger, peeled and very thinly sliced
4 tbsp soy sauce
4 tbsp dry sherry
1 tsp sugar

1 tbsp lemon juice
1 tbsp cornflour
225 ml/8 fl oz lamb or chicken stock
3 tbsp oil
1 tsp sesame oil
1 garlic clove
1 bunch spring onions, cut in 2.5-cm/1-in lengths

■ Place the lamb in a dish and mix in the ginger. Stir the soy sauce, sherry, sugar and lemon juice together, then pour the mixture over the lamb and ginger. Cover and leave to marinate for several hours.
■ Blend the cornflour to a smooth paste with a little of the stock, then stir in the remaining stock. Heat the oils, add the garlic and use a slotted spoon to add the lamb and ginger to the pan. Stir-fry the lamb until browned, then add the spring onions and continue stir-frying for 2 minutes.
■ Pour the marinade juices from the lamb and the stock. Bring to the boil and simmer, stirring, for 5 minutes. Taste for seasoning before serving, adding a little extra soy sauce if necessary.

LAMB WITH BLACK BEAN SALSA

BRAZIL

*In this Brazilian-inspired dish, a leg of lamb is marinated, then roasted
or barbecued, and served with a spicy salsa. It is a fairly easy dish
that requires a minimum of last-minute work.*

SERVES 6

leg of lamb, about
  2.25 kg/5 lb
4 tbsp olive oil
3 tbsp red wine vinegar
2 tbsp fresh orange juice
4 garlic cloves, crushed
1 tsp dried oregano
½ tsp dried rosemary
50 g/2 oz finely chopped
  onion

BLACK BEAN SALSA
450-g/1-lb can black or
  kidney beans, rinsed
  and drained
50 g/2 oz chopped sweet
  red pepper
3 spring onions, chopped
2 chipotle chillies, minced
3 tbsp chopped fresh
  coriander
1½ tsp chopped fresh
  oregano or ½ tsp dried
1 tbsp olive oil
2 tbsp fresh lime juice

■ Put the lamb in a non-metallic dish. To make a
marinade, combine all the remaining ingredients
except the salsa. Pour the marinade over the lamb,
making sure that the entire surface is coated. Marinate
the lamb in the refrigerator for at least 2 hours and up
to 24 hours, turning it occasionally.

■ Roast the lamb in a 180°C/350°F/Gas Mark 4 oven or
over a grill – about 20 minutes per 450 g/1 lb in the
oven, considerably less time on a grill. Lamb is
traditionally served rare or medium rare. It is easier to
carve if it is allowed to rest for about 20 minutes after it
comes out of the oven.

■ While the lamb is roasting, make the salsa. Combine
all the ingredients, then taste and adjust the seasoning.
Serve with the lamb.

STEWED LAMB SINT MAARTEN

NETHERLANDS ANTILLES

Traditionally, this dish is made with goat. This lamb version is even more delicious. Serve it with rice, mashed potatoes or noodles and a minted vegetable.

SERVES 4–6

2 tbsp vegetable oil
900 g/2 lb boneless lamb, cut into 5-cm/2-in cubes
2 medium onions, chopped
4 garlic cloves, chopped
50 g/2 oz celery, chopped
1 tsp finely chopped root ginger
3 tbsp minced habañero peppers or hot pepper sauce
1 small green pepper, chopped

2 medium tomatoes, skinned and chopped
1 tbsp lime or lemon juice
1 tsp ground cumin
1 tsp ground allspice
125–175 ml/4–6 fl oz beer
1 tbsp red wine vinegar
1 large cucumber, peeled and chopped
40 g/1½ oz stoned green olives (optional)
1 tbsp capers (optional)

■ Heat the oil in a large, heavy-based saucepan over medium-high heat. Brown the lamb in the oil, then remove and drain. Add the onions, garlic, celery, ginger, hot peppers or hot pepper sauce and green pepper and sauté until the onions are soft.

■ Combine the lamb, onion mixture, tomatoes, lime or lemon juice, cumin and allspice and cover with beer. Simmer until the meat is very tender and starts to fall apart, about 1½ hours. Add more beer if necessary.

■ Add the vinegar, cucumber and olives and capers, if using, and simmer for 15 minutes before serving.

MINCE KEBABS

LEBANON

Variations of mince 'rolls' are found all over the Middle East, Greece, Turkey and the Balkan states, and are well known in the West from their frequent appearance on 'kebab house' menus. What distinguishes the national versions are the spicing and special ingredients. This Lebanese recipe is satisfying but simple.

SERVES 6–8

4 slices bread, crusts
  removed and cubed
  (about 150 g/5 oz)
1 garlic clove, crushed
900 g/2 lb minced lamb
2 small onions, grated
1½ tsp ground cumin

½ tsp cayenne pepper
3 tbsp finely chopped
  parsley
1 egg
salt and freshly ground
  pepper
lemon wedges

■ Place the bread cubes in a small bowl and add enough water to dampen them – about 4 to 5 tablespoons. Add the garlic and, using your hands, mash the bread and garlic with the water. Leave to stand for about 10 minutes.

■ In a large bowl, again using your hands, mix together the lamb, onion, cumin, cayenne and parsley. Knead in the bread paste, the egg and seasoning to taste, until everything is mixed and the meat has absorbed the liquid and become drier and smoother.

■ With your hands, roll the meat into 6 to 8 long cylinders. Pass a skewer through each cylinder and pat the meat around to secure it.

■ Cook the kebabs over grey-ashed coals for about 20 minutes, until they are brown on all sides. Alternatively, cook under a hot grill, turning two or three times, until done. Serve the kebabs with the lemon wedges.

LAMB PILAF

RUSSIA

There are numerous pilaf recipes originating in Central Asia; this one from Russia utilizes the rich bounty of fruit which grows there – the apples are particularly famous.

SERVES 6

50 g/2 oz blanched
   flaked almonds
4 tbsp vegetable oil
450 g/1 lb lamb steaks,
   cubed
2 large carrots, cut into
   julienne strips
2 large onions, thinly
   sliced
75 g/3 oz dried apricots,
   chopped

50 g/2 oz raisins
700 g/1½ lb long-grain
   white rice
salt and freshly ground
   black pepper
450 ml/¾ pt chicken stock
150 ml/¼ pt orange juice
1 tsp grated orange rind
600 ml/1 pt water
1 medium red apple,
   cored and chopped

■ Preheat the oven to 200°C/400°F/Gas Mark 6. Scatter the almonds on a baking sheet and toast in the oven until golden, about 5 minutes. Set aside and turn the oven down to 180°C/350°F/Gas Mark 4.

■ Heat the oil in a large frying pan over medium-high heat. When just smoking, add the lamb cubes and sauté for 6 minutes, or until well browned. Transfer the meat with a slotted spoon to a large casserole.

■ Turn the heat down slightly and sauté the carrots in the oil for 3 minutes, stirring, then add the onions and continue to sauté for another 6 minutes, until the onions are soft and lightly coloured. Stir in the dried apricots, raisins and rice. Cook for 2 minutes until the rice is coated with the oil and is becoming opaque.

■ Add the rice mixture to the casserole with the meat. Season to taste, then pour in the chicken stock, orange juice and rind, and water. Bring to the boil, then cover the casserole and transfer it to the oven. Bake for 40 minutes, or until all the liquid is absorbed.

■ Remove the pilaf from the oven, stir in the chopped apple, and transfer it to a large serving dish, making a neat mound. Scatter the toasted almonds over the top and serve.

MINTED LAMB WITH VEGETABLES

UNITED KINGDOM

SERVES 4

450 g/1 lb lean boneless
  lamb, diced
2 tbsp plain flour
salt and freshly ground
  black pepper
2 tbsp oil
knob of butter
225 g/8 oz small pickling
  onions
900 g/2 lb small new
  potatoes, boiled until
  tender

225 g/8 oz mange-tout
225 g/8 fl oz dry white
  wine
4 tbsp chopped fresh mint
1 head endive, roughly
  shredded, to serve
mint sprigs to garnish

■ Toss the lamb with the flour and seasoning. Heat the oil and butter, then stir-fry the onions for about 10 minutes, until they are lightly browned. Add the meat and stir-fry for a further 8 to 10 minutes, until both meat and onions are browned and the onions are tender.

■ Stir in the potatoes and mange-tout and continue to stir-fry for 5 minutes or so, until the potatoes are hot and the mange-tout are lightly cooked. Pour in the wine and bring to the boil. Boil rapidly, stirring, for 2 minutes, so that the ingredients are coated in a lightly thickened glaze. Taste and adjust the seasoning.

■ Stir in the mint just before turning the lamb mixture out on to a bed of endive, either on one large dish or on individual plates. Garnish with mint sprigs.

BRAISED LAMB

PUERTO RICO

SERVES 6

6 lamb chops
3 tbsp honey
2 tbsp dry sherry
50 ml/2 fl oz soy sauce
2 tbsp white vinegar

2 garlic cloves, crushed
50 ml/2 fl oz chicken
   stock
2 tsp brown sugar
2 tbsp dark rum

■ Place the lamb chops in a glass bowl. Mix all the remaining ingredients together and pour over the chops. Refrigerate overnight.

■ Put the chops and marinade in an ovenproof dish and cover with foil or a lid. Bake in a preheated 180°C/350°F/Gas Mark 4 oven for 45 minutes, then serve at once with baked cassava or breadfruit.

LAMB KEBABS

GREECE

These are small skewers of meat traditionally cooked over charcoal and served as a snack, starter, main course or as part of an array of Meze dishes. The lemon is the secret ingredient in this classic dish, so make sure it is freshly squeezed.

SERVES 4–6

3 tbsp olive oil
3 tbsp freshly squeezed
   lemon juice
2 tsp dried thyme
2 garlic cloves, crushed
freshly ground black
   pepper, to taste

1 kg/2¼ lb lean lamb, cut
   into 2.5-cm/1-in cubes
6 bay leaves
wedges of lemon, to serve

■ To make the marinade, mix together the olive oil, lemon juice, thyme, garlic and freshly ground black pepper in a screw-top jar. Secure the lid and shake well to combine the ingredients.

■ Place the cubed lamb in a shallow dish. Crumble 2 bay leaves and sprinkle over the meat. Pour the marinade over the meat and stir to coat evenly. Cover and refrigerate for 2 hours.

■ Thread the remaining bay leaves on to four metal skewers, then divide the meat between them. Cook the kebabs under a preheated grill for about 5 to 10 minutes, or until they are cooked through. Brush with the reserved marinade and turn the kebabs during cooking. Serve with lemon wedges.

BAKED PAPAYA WITH MEAT FILLING

JAMAICA

SERVES 6

2 tbsp vegetable oil
1 small onion, finely chopped
1 garlic clove, crushed
450 g/1 lb lean minced beef or lamb
4 ripe tomatoes, skinned and chopped
2 chillies for a hot dish or ½ thinly chopped fresh hot pepper for a mild flavour

1 tsp salt
freshly ground black pepper
2.25 kg/5 lb green papaya, halved and seeded
25 g/1 oz cheese, grated

■ Preheat the oven to 180°C/350°F/Gas Mark 4. Heat the oil in a large frying pan and fry the onion and garlic in it for 5 minutes. Then stir in the beef or lamb and cook until browned.

■ Add the tomatoes, hot pepper, salt and freshly ground black pepper to taste. Continue to cook until all the liquid has evaporated.

■ Spoon the meat mixture into the papaya shells and place them in a shallow roasting tin. Pour in enough boiling water around them to come about 2.5 cm/1 in up the sides of the shells when they are placed side by side. Bake in the preheated oven for 1 hour. Sprinkle with half the grated cheese and bake for another 30 minutes. Serve sprinkled with the remaining cheese.

SAUTÉED LAMB WITH AUBERGINE

VIETNAM

SERVES 4

2 large aubergines, ends
  cut off, thickly sliced
salt
3 tbsp olive oil
8 lamb cutlets, trimmed
2 garlic cloves, crushed
6 large tomatoes,
  blanched, skinned and
  thickly sliced
freshly ground black
  pepper

GARNISH
1 lemon, sliced
sprigs of mint

SAUCE
2 tbsp fresh mint, chopped
150 ml/¼ pt natural
  yoghurt
freshly ground black
  pepper

■ Spread out the aubergine on a work surface,
sprinkle with salt and leave for 20 minutes. Rinse the
aubergine and dry with kitchen paper.

■ Heat 2 tablespoons olive oil in a wok over a very
high heat and add the lamb cutlets. When brown, lower
the heat and continue cooking until the meat is tender
– about 5 minutes on each side. Remove from the wok,
drain on kitchen paper and keep in a warm oven.

■ Add the remaining oil to the wok and fry the
aubergine slices with the garlic until they are lightly
browned on both sides. (If the oil dries out, add a little
more.) When cooked, push the aubergine up the side
of the wok and add the tomato slices. Stir-fry for a few
moments and season with salt and pepper. Place the
vegetables on a dish and arrange the cutlets over them.
Garnish with lemon slices and sprigs of mint.

■ Prepare the sauce by stirring the mint into the
yoghurt. Grind some black pepper over it and serve in a
small bowl.

SEAFOOD

PASTA WITH SALMON, DILL AND MUSTARD

———— ITALY ————

Although delicate, salmon is a rich fish and the piquancy of this mustard sauce complements it perfectly. For classic simplicity, arrange the fish and its dressing on fresh egg noodles. The dill must be fresh – forget the recipe when you have only dried dill as it will make the sauce taste as though you have used grass cuttings.

SERVES 4

700–900 g/1½–2 lb
  salmon fillet, skinned
salt and freshly ground
  black pepper
4 tbsp olive oil
1 tbsp lemon juice
½ onion, finely chopped
2 tbsp flour
150 ml/¼ pt milk

4 tbsp Dijon mustard or
  other mild mustard
300 ml/½ pt soured cream
3 tbsp chopped dill
350-450 g/12–16 oz
  fresh tagliatelle
¼ cucumber, peeled and
  finely diced
1 celery stick, finely diced

■ Lay the salmon on a large piece of double-thick foil. Season it really well, then sprinkle with 1 tablespoon of the oil and the lemon juice. Grill the fish for about 15 minutes, or until cooked through.

■ Meanwhile, heat the remaining oil in a saucepan and add the onion. Cook, stirring, for 10 minutes. Stir in the flour and cook for 3 minutes before stirring in the milk, then bring to the boil. Beat the mustard into the thick sauce, then stir in the cream and heat gently but do not boil. Finally, stir in the dill and remove from the heat, then taste for seasoning.

■ Bring a large pan of salted water to a rolling boil, then add the pasta and cook for 3 or 4 minutes, until *al dente*.

■ Mix the cucumber and celery. Drain the cooking liquid from the salmon into the sauce. Use two forks to separate the cooked salmon into large chunks.

■ Drain the pasta, return it to the pan, then mix in the mustard and dill sauce. Lightly stir in the fish. Divide between serving platters and top each portion with a little of the cucumber and celery.

RED MULLET WITH GARLIC

———— GREECE ————

SERVES 6

6 tbsp very finely chopped
  fresh parsley
6 garlic cloves, crushed
salt and freshly ground
  black pepper, to taste
6 red mullet, cleaned

flour, for coating
olive oil, for shallow frying
chopped fresh parsley, to
  garnish
lemon wedges to serve

■ In a small bowl, combine the parsley with the garlic and season with salt and freshly ground black pepper. Place about 1 teaspoon of the garlic mixture in the cavity of each fish and rub any remaining mixture evenly over the skins. Coat the fish lightly and evenly with the flour.

■ Heat the oil in a deep frying pan and cook the fish, no more than two at a time, for about 5 to 7 minutes, or until crisp on the outside and cooked through. Using a slotted spoon, transfer to a dish lined with kitchen paper to drain. Sprinkle with parsley and serve with lemon wedges.

HERRING, MEAT AND BEETROOT SALAD

RUSSIA

*This is a signature dish of Russian cuisine. It makes a delicious
lunch dish on a warm summer's day.*

SERVES 8

3 tsp dry mustard powder
½ tsp sugar
300 ml/½ pt whipping
  cream
5 large boiled beetroot,
  peeled and diced
2 tart apples, cored,
  peeled and diced
6 large potatoes, boiled,
  peeled and diced
2 sweet-sour Polish-style
  gherkins, diced

2 fillets of pickled herring,
  drained and diced
450 g/1 lb leftover lean
  cooked beef or pork,
  trimmed and diced
salt and freshly ground
  black pepper
2–3 tbsp dry white wine
2 hard-boiled eggs,
  chopped
lettuce leaves, washed

■ To make the dressing, combine the mustard, sugar
and whipping cream in a large bowl. By hand or with
an electric mixer, whip the mustard cream until it holds
soft peaks. Set aside.

■ In another large bowl, combine the beetroot, apples,
potatoes, gherkins, herrings, meat, seasoning to taste,
and the wine. Toss to combine, then gently fold in the
hard-boiled eggs and three-quarters of the dressing.
Chill for 30 minutes, then transfer the salad to a lettuce-
lined plate or glass bowl and top with the remaining
whipped cream.

RED SNAPPER WITH GREEN SAUCE

MEXICO

This is a Jewish-Mexican recipe, which involves baking fish or chicken in a vegetable and herb purée 'blanket' to keep the flesh moist and tender.

SERVES 6

vegetable oil for greasing
1.5–1.8 kg/3–4 lb red
  snapper or sea bass
  fillets
fresh juice of 5 limes
salt and freshly ground
  black pepper

SAUCE
1 head cos lettuce,
  trimmed, cored and
  shredded
½ cucumber, peeled and
  seeded
1 small green pepper,
  cored, seeded and
  chopped

1 red onion, quartered
3–4 garlic cloves
1 small bunch watercress,
  stems trimmed
4–5 spring onions,
  trimmed
25 g/1 oz coriander
  leaves

GARNISH
cherry tomatoes
ripe olives
chopped fresh coriander
  leaves

■ Lightly grease a deep baking dish. Place fish in centre of dish and rub with a little lime juice. Sprinkle with salt and pepper to taste. Set aside.

■ Make the sauce. In a food processor fitted with metal blade, process the lettuce, cucumber, green pepper, red onion, garlic, watercress, spring onions and coriander leaves with the remaining lime juice. Pour sauce over fish, cover and refrigerate at least 2 hours.

■ Preheat oven to 180°C/350°F/Gas Mark 4. Uncover fish and bake, basting twice, until fish is opaque and flesh flakes when pierced with a knife, 20 to 25 minutes. Remove fish to serving platter. Pour sauce over and garnish with cherry tomatoes, olives and coriander.

PRAWN CREOLE

JAMAICA

The liquid in this version of Prawn Creole is reduced until the sauce becomes quite thick and flavourful. The water chestnuts add a crunchy Oriental texture.

SERVES 4–6

2 tbsp vegetable oil
1 large onion, chopped
8 garlic cloves, crushed
2 large celery sticks, finely
  chopped
4 medium tomatoes,
  chopped
2 medium green peppers,
  chopped
2 tbsp tomato purée
1 tsp hot pepper sauce
½ tsp dried oregano
1 tsp dried thyme
2 tsp Worcestershire sauce

1.5 ltr/2½ pt chicken stock
750 g/1½ lb prawns,
  shelled and deveined
225-g/8-oz can sliced
  water chestnuts, drained
  and rinsed, or 225 g/
  8 oz jicama, sliced
½ tbsp lime juice
salt and freshly ground
  black pepper
700 g/1½ lb cooked long-
  grain rice
1 tbsp finely chopped
  coriander or parsley, to
  garnish

■ Heat the oil in a large saucepan, frying pan or wok. Add the onion, garlic, celery, tomatoes and peppers and fry over moderate heat until tender. Then add the tomato purée, hot pepper sauce, oregano and thyme and blend, stirring constantly, for about 2 minutes. Add the Worcestershire sauce and chicken stock and bring to the boil over medium-high heat until thickened, about 30 minutes. Add the prawns and water chestnuts and simmer, uncovered, until the prawns are opaque throughout, about 4 minutes. Remove from the heat and adjust the seasoning with more hot pepper sauce to taste, lime juice and salt and pepper. Serve immediately, over or under a scoop of rice, on warm dishes and sprinkle the top with coriander or parsley.

FETTUCINE WITH PRAWNS AND CHILLI-CREAM SAUCE

ITALY

SERVES 4

75 g/3 oz butter
350 g/12 oz medium to large prawns, cleaned
450 g/1 lb fettucine
225 ml/8 fl oz double cream
½ tsp salt
pinch of white pepper
50 g/2 oz grated Parmesan cheese, plus extra for garnish

ROAST JALAPEÑO SALSA

15 jalapeño chillies
4 Anaheim chillies
3 slices red onion, peeled, about 1 cm/½ in thick
5 garlic cloves, unpeeled
¼ tsp dried oregano
2 tbsp olive oil
1 tbsp fresh lemon juice
¼ tsp salt

■ Make the salsa first. Cut all the chillies in half, and remove the seeds and veins. Grill the chillies, onion slices and garlic over a barbecue or under a grill, remembering to keep the skins of the chillies facing the heat source. They will cook unevenly, but it's not necessary for the skins to be completely blackened; they must, however, be charred through to the flesh. Remove them from the heat when they are ready and seal in a plastic bag for 10 minutes. This will loosen the skins and make them easier to remove.

■ The onion slices should soften and brown slightly. Turn and cook them on both sides. Turn the garlic once and cook until softened. Garlic will turn bitter if charred, so watch it closely.

■ With a sharp knife, peel and scrape the skins off the chillies. Jalapeño skins are not as tough as those of many other chillies, so it's all right to leave part of the skin on. Roast chillies tend to become stringy, so cut them in strips from side to side, not lengthwise. Put the strips in a food processor.

■ Cut each onion slice into quarters and add them to the food processor. Peel the garlic, trim off any burned spots and add that too. Add remaining ingredients and process until they are well chopped but not a paste. The mixture will be fairly dry.

■ Melt 25 g/1 oz butter in a large frying pan. Add 1 tablespoon jalapeño salsa and cook for 1 minute, stirring. Add the prawns and sauté until they curl tightly and are an opaque white-pink, 2 to 3 minutes. Remove them with a slotted spoon and set aside.

■ Cook the fettucine in plenty of boiling salted water until just tender, then drain. While the pasta is cooking, add the remaining butter to the frying pan in which you cooked the prawns. When it is melted and foamy, add the remaining salsa. Cook, stirring, for 1 minute, then add the cream, salt and white pepper, and cook until the sauce thickens slightly, about 3 minutes. Stir in the prawns, then stir in the Parmesan cheese and the cooked, drained noodles. Toss until the noodles are coated. Serve with Parmesan sprinkled on top.

CRAB-STUFFED COURGETTES

————— UNITED STATES —————

Fresh crabmeat is mixed with sautéed vegetables, herbs and breadcrumbs, then stuffed into hollowed-out courgette halves. In Louisiana, the dish is called pirogues, after the dugout canoes used in the bayous, which they resemble. You can also try this filling in mirliton – also known as chayote – another squash popular in some parts of the South. Depending on the size of the courgette, one boat can be a main course.

SERVES 4–8

4 thick courgettes	1 tsp dried basil
3 tbsp vegetable oil	½ tsp dried thyme
75 g/3 oz onion, chopped	1 tsp salt
	¼ tsp black pepper
75 g/3 oz celery, chopped	¼ tsp cayenne pepper
	2–3 tbsp milk or clam juice
40 g/1½ oz green pepper, chopped	350 g/12 oz fresh crabmeat
2 garlic cloves, finely chopped	Parmesan cheese
75 g/3 oz dry breadcrumbs	

■ Preheat oven to 180°C/350°F/Gas Mark 4. Lightly grease a large, shallow baking dish.
■ Cut the courgettes in half lengthways. Scoop out the pulp, leaving a 5-mm/¼-in shell. Chop the pulp. Sauté it in the vegetable oil with the onion, celery, green pepper and garlic until the vegetables are tender and excess moisture has evaporated, 10 to 12 minutes. Remove vegetables from the heat.
■ In a large bowl, mix the breadcrumbs, herbs and spices, and cooked vegetables. Add enough milk or clam juice so that the mixture is moist, but not mushy.
■ With your fingers, pick through the crabmeat to remove any bits of bone or cartilage. Gently mix it into the stuffing. Mound the stuffing into the courgette shells. Sprinkle with Parmesan cheese. Place the courgettes in the prepared dish and bake until they are tender, about 20 minutes. Serve immediately.

DRUNKEN SQUID

————— MEXICO —————

This recipe uses only the outer envelope of the squid. You can buy prepared squid, but preparing them yourself is easy (and less unpleasant) than it looks. Salt your hands to get a good grip; grasp the tentacles in one hand and the body in the other, and pull them apart. The tentacles will pull away, complete with the entrails. Feed the tentacles to the cat.

SERVES 6

900 g/2 lb squid	250 ml/8 fl oz red wine
125 ml/4 fl oz brandy	salt and pepper
1.5 ltr/2½ pt tomato salsa (see page 24)	olives and capers for garnish

■ Clean the squid with plenty of salt. Pound it thoroughly with a rolling-pin, then marinade for 1 hour (or more) in the brandy.
■ Add just enough water to cover the squid; bring to the boil and simmer gently until tender. Drain, reserving the broth. Cut the squid into 1–2.5-cm (½–1-in) squares.
■ Mix the broth, the tomato sauce and the wine. Add pepper and salt. Simmer the squid in this for another ½ hour. Garnish with olives and capers.

MUSSEL PANCAKES

SPAIN

Galician mussels are the best in the world, and this simple recipe shows them off perfectly. The thin crêpes are related to the ones made in Brittany, which shares the same Celtic culture.

SERVES 4

1.75 kg/4 lb mussels	CRÊPE BATTER
125 ml/4 fl oz dry white wine	100 g/3½ oz flour
2 tbsp chopped onion	2 large eggs
4 parsley stalks, bruised	mussel liquor (see method)
6 black peppercorns, crushed	4–6 tbsp thick cream
	about 4 tbsp butter
	6 tbsp chopped parsley

■ Wash the mussels, discarding any that are open (and do not close when touched). Pull off the beards. Put the wine, onion, parsley stalks and peppercorns in a big pan and bring to a simmer. Add the mussels (in 2 batches) and cover tightly. Cook over a high heat for 3 to 4 minutes, shaking occasionally, until they are open. Discard the shells and any that remain shut or smell strongly. Strain the liquid into a measuring jug and leave to cool. Taste for seasoning.

■ Make the crêpe batter. Put the flour in a bowl or blender and work in the eggs, mussel liquor and 2 tablespoons of cream. (Don't overbeat in a blender.) Let the batter stand, if you can, for 1 hour.

■ Melt 1¼ tablespoons of butter in a frying pan, swirling it round. Add to the batter and stir thoroughly. Heat another ½ tablespoon of butter and swirl. Use about 100 ml/3 fl oz batter per crêpe: it is easier to pour from a cup. Lift the pan and pour the batter fast into the middle of it, tilting the pan so the batter covers the base. (If you overdo the liquid, spoon off anything that doesn't set at once: crêpes should be thin.)

■ Put the pan back over the heat, shaking it to make sure the crêpe does not stick. Cook for a minute until golden underneath, then flip over with a fish slice (picking up with fingers is just as easy). Briefly fry the other side. Roll and keep warm on a plate while you make more.

■ Warm the remaining cream in a saucepan with the mussel bodies. Spoon the mussels and a little cream on to one edge of a pancake, sprinkle with the parsley and roll up. Do not keep them waiting long.

CALYPSO COD STEAKS

BARBADOS

These cod steaks have zip, thanks to the hot peppers. Salmon works well, too, but do not use salted cod in this dish.

SERVES 6

3 tbsp fresh lime juice	6 cod or salmon steaks,
2 tbsp olive oil	2 cm/¾ in thick and
2 tsp crushed garlic	weighing about
1 tsp crushed hot pepper or 2 tsp hot pepper sauce	175 g/6 oz each

■ In a bowl, whisk together the lime juice, olive oil, garlic and hot pepper or hot pepper sauce.

■ Brush the grill rack with oil and preheat the grill. Grill the fish steaks for about 10 to 12 minutes on one side, basting frequently with the sauce, then turn and cook on the other side for another 10 to 12 minutes, again basting frequently, until done but not overcooked.

SWEET-AND-SOUR FISH

ISRAEL

In Eastern Europe, sweet-and-sour fish is generally prepared with carp. In France it is known as carpe à la Juive (Jewish-style carp) and it was traditional to serve the head of the fish to the head of the house at Jewish New Year. This recipe uses fish steaks rather than a whole fish.

SERVES 6

6 fish steaks, such as carp, pike, salmon or trout, 2.5 cm/1 in thick (1.5 kg/3 lb total weight)
salt and freshly ground black pepper
1 onion, thinly sliced
1 carrot, thinly sliced
1 bay leaf
4–6 whole cloves
1 lemon, sliced and pips removed

2–4 slices fresh root ginger
1 tbsp black peppercorns
125 ml/4 fl oz red wine vinegar
125 g/4 oz light brown sugar
75 g/3 oz raisins
4 ginger biscuits, crushed to crumbs (optional)
3–4 tbsp chopped fresh parsley
lemon twists for garnish

■ Rinse fish steaks under cold running water and pat dry with kitchen paper. Sprinkle lightly with salt and pepper to taste, then set aside.

■ In a large, non-aluminium deep frying pan combine the onion, carrot, bay leaf, cloves, lemon slices, root ginger and peppercorns with 900 ml/1½ pt cold water. Over high heat, bring to a boil, then simmer, covered, for 15 minutes.

■ Add fish steaks and cook over medium-low heat, covered, until fish pulls away from centre bone and turns opaque, 10 to 12 minutes. Using a fish slice, carefully transfer fish steaks to a large, deep glass or ceramic baking dish.

■ Bring cooking liquid to a boil again and boil until reduced by half, 7 to 10 minutes. Strain into a smaller saucepan and add the vinegar, brown sugar and raisins. Simmer 2 to 3 minutes longer, stir in the ginger biscuit crumbs, if using, and chopped parsley. Cool slightly, then pour over the fish. Cool completely, then refrigerate overnight. Serve chilled, garnished with lemon twists.

STIR-FRIED SEAFOOD WITH MINT, GARLIC AND CHILLIES

VIETNAM

SERVES 4

125 g/4 oz fish fillets
6 mussels
1 small uncooked crab, cleaned and chopped
125 g/4 oz squid pieces
125 g/4 oz uncooked prawns
125 g/4 oz scallops
2 garlic cloves, chopped
2 large fresh chilli peppers, chopped
1 tbsp chopped coriander root

1 tbsp vegetable oil
2 tbsp oyster sauce
2 tbsp Nuoc Mam sauce or light soy sauce and 1 tsp anchovy sauce, mixed well
1 sweet pepper, cut in strips
1 onion, thinly sliced
2 shallots, thinly sliced
4 tbsp chopped fresh mint

■ Wash and prepare the seafood. Cut the fish fillets into bite-sized pieces. Scrub the mussels and remove the beards. Take the limbs off the crab and crack the shell with a hammer so the meat is easy to remove at the table. Remove the outer shell, clean out the crab body and break into bite-sized pieces. Set aside.

■ Put the garlic, chillies and coriander root in a blender and make a coarse paste. Heat the oil and fry the paste over medium heat. Add the seafood and stir-fry gently so the fish fillet does not break up. Add the oyster sauce and Nuoc Mam sauce. Taste, cover and simmer for a few minutes.

■ Remove the lid and add the sweet pepper, onion, shallots and mint and stir-fry gently (the fish fillets are now even more delicate) for a couple of minutes, then remove from the heat. Arrange on a large, shallow serving dish and garnish with whatever herbs you happen to have. Serve with steaming rice.

LAKE FISH IN MUSTARD SAUCE

—— RUSSIA ——

*Omul is a delicious relative of the salmon, found only in Lake Baikal, one of
the most beautiful lakes and on record as the deepest (1.6 km/1 mile)
in the world.*

SERVES 6

2 tbsp sunflower oil
1.5 kg/3 lb salmon fillet,
  washed and dried
2½ tbsp German-style
  mustard
1½ tbsp honey
grated rind and juice of ½
  small lemon

1 tbsp finely chopped fresh
  dill
salt and freshly ground
  black pepper
dill sprigs

■ If you are grilling the fish, brush a sheet of foil with a little sunflower oil before placing the salmon skin-side down on it. Whether grilling or barbecuing, place the fish (and foil, if used) on a baking tray. Mix together the remaining oil, mustard, honey, lemon rind and juice, seasoning and chopped dill. Brush the fish liberally with the mixture.

■ Preheat a grill to hot. (If you are using a barbecue, the coals should be greying. Place the fish in a fish holder and turn it flesh-side down towards the coals.) Grill or barbecue the fish about 13 cm/5 in from the heat for about 10 minutes, or until slightly translucent. Transfer to a serving platter and garnish with dill sprigs before serving.

SEAFOOD LASAGNE

ITALY

SERVES 6

350 g/12 oz fresh
   lasagne verdi
2 tbsp olive oil
25 g/1 oz butter
1 onion, finely chopped
1 bay leaf
40 g/1½ oz plain flour
300 ml/½ pt dry white
   wine
300 ml/½ pt fish stock
125 g/4 oz button
   mushrooms, sliced
salt and freshly ground
   black pepper

700 g/1½ lb white fish
   fillet, skinned and cut
   into chunks
225 g/8 oz peeled
   cooked prawns, thawed
   if frozen
450 g/1 lb mussels,
   cooked and shelled (see
   page 147)
2 tbsp chopped parsley
1 quantity béchamel sauce
   (see page 31)
50 g/2 oz Cheddar
   cheese, grated

■ Lower the pieces of pasta one at a time into a large saucepan of boiling salted water. Bring back to the boil and cook for 3 minutes. Drain and rinse under cold water. Lay the pasta on double-thick sheets of kitchen paper.

■ Set the oven at 180°C/350°F/Gas Mark 4. Heat the oil and butter in a saucepan and add the onion and bay leaf. Cook for 10 minutes, until the onion is softened slightly, then stir in the flour. Slowly pour in the wine and stock and bring to the boil, stirring all the time. Add the mushrooms and seasoning, then simmer for 10 minutes. Remove from the heat before stirring in the fish, prawns, mussels and parsley. Layer this fish sauce and the lasagne in a large ovenproof dish, ending with a layer of lasagne. Pour the béchamel sauce evenly over the pasta, then sprinkle the cheese on top. Bake for 40 to 50 minutes, until golden brown and bubbling hot.

MIXED FISH AND SHELLFISH STEW

SPAIN

SERVES 6–8

1.25 kg/2½ lb mixed fish,
   cleaned
5 tbsp olive oil
700 g/1½ lb onions,
   chopped
450 g/1 lb clams, mussels
   etc., cleaned
salt and freshly ground
   black pepper
1½ tbsp paprika

10 black peppercorns,
   crushed
½ dried chilli, seeded and
   chopped
freshly grated nutmeg
8–10 tbsp chopped
   parsley
350 g/12 oz small
   prawns in their shells
450 ml/¾ pt dry white
   wine

■ Cut off the spines and fins from the fish with scissors and remove all scales by stroking the fish from the tail to the head with the back of a knife or your thumbs. Rinse the fish inside and cut off heads (freeze to use for stock). Cut whole fish across into sections about 5 cm/ 2 in long, and cut fillets into similar-sized pieces.

■ Warm 2 tablespoons of oil in the bottom of your chosen pot. Put in a good bed of onions. On this arrange a layer of one-third of the fish, choosing from the different varieties. Pack half the clams or mussels into all the spaces. Season with salt, ½ tablespoon of paprika, half the peppercorns, a little ground pepper, chilli and the nutmeg. Sprinkle with 1 tablespoon of oil and plenty of parsley. Make a bed of prawns on top.

■ Repeat all the layers. Make a top layer of fish, seasoning as before and packing onion into the gaps. Add more parsley. Add the wine and about 200 ml/ 7 fl oz of water to almost cover. Then re-season the top layer, adding ½ tablespoon of paprika and another tablespoon of oil

■ Bring to simmering (the best part of 10 minutes), then cover, turn down the heat and simmer for 15 minutes. Check the broth seasoning, and serve with crusty bread. (Take the prawn heads off before eating them, if you wish.)

CREOLE-STYLE MARINATED FISH

JAMAICA

SERVES 4

600 ml/1 pt water
6 tbsp fresh lime or lemon
  juice
2 tsp salt
900 g/2 lb firm fish (such
  as snapper or mullet),
  scaled, cleaned and cut
  into 4 steaks, 225 g/
  8 oz each
3 tbsp vegetable oil mixed
  with 1 tsp liquid annatto
125 g/4 oz spring onions,
  chopped

4 garlic cloves, chopped
½ hot pepper, finely
  chopped
3 ripe tomatoes, skinned
  and chopped
1 tsp thyme
1 bay leaf
4 parsley sprigs
freshly ground black
  pepper
2 tbsp olive oil

■ Put 450 ml/¾ pt of the water plus the lime or lemon juice and salt into a large, shallow, glass dish and stir until the salt dissolves. Wash the fish steaks under cold running water and marinate them in the lime or lemon juice mixture for 1 hour.

■ Remove the fish from the marinade. Heat the annatto-flavoured oil in a large saucepan over a medium heat. Add the spring onions, garlic and hot pepper and cook until soft.

■ Add the tomatoes, thyme, bay leaf, parsley and freshly ground black pepper and simmer for 10 minutes. Stir in the remaining water, add the fish and bring to the boil. Reduce the heat and simmer for 10 more minutes. Preheat the oven to 190°C/375°F/Gas Mark 5.

■ Transfer the fish and sauce to a heated baking dish. Sprinkle over the olive oil and bake in the preheated oven for 5 minutes.

FLAT FISH WITH HAZELNUT AND CHILLI SAUCE

──── SPAIN ────

Simply fried, flat fish are a treat when moist and slightly underdone. Small, whole fish cooked on the bone are best, but fillets may be easier.

SERVES 4

4 small lemon sole, about 200–275 g/7–9 oz each, cleaned, or 4 plaice fillets
2–3 tbsp flour
salt and ground white pepper
2–4 tbsp butter
1–2 tbsp olive oil

SAUCE
25 g/1 oz blanched almonds
25 g/1 oz blanched hazelnuts

2 garlic cloves, finely chopped
4–6 tbsp olive oil
1 slice stale bread
1 big ripe tomato, skinned and seeded
½ dried chilli or ½ jalapeño chilli, seeded and chopped
salt and freshly ground black pepper
2 tsp red wine vinegar
4 tbsp fino sherry

■ Start the sauce by toasting the nuts in a low oven (160°C/320°F/Gas Mark 3) for 20 minutes until biscuit-coloured. Fry the garlic, then the bread slice in 4 tablespoons of oil and reserve. Add the chopped tomatoes and chilli or cayenne pepper to the pan and cook, stirring until the mixture has thickened. Season.
■ Grind the nuts in a blender. Add the bread, garlic, vinegar and sherry and pulverize everything. Stir this into the tomato sauce. Check the seasoning.
■ If you wish, the whole sauce can be blended once more to a pink 'mayonnaise'; this makes a better salad dressing. Add a little extra oil for this second blending.
■ Strip the dark skin off the sole, if you prefer. Dust with seasoned flour. Heat 2 tablespoons of butter and 1 tablespoon of oil in a frying pan. When very hot, put in the fish. Whole fish need 3 to 4 minutes for the first side, 2 minutes for the second, fillets about 2 minutes each side. Serve on hot plates and pass the sauce round in a bowl.

CRAB AND COURGETTE SALAD

──── ITALY ────

SERVES 4

225 g/8 oz fresh pasta shapes
225 g/8 oz small, young courgettes
6 spring onions, chopped
6 basil sprigs
salt and freshly ground black pepper

2 tbsp lemon juice
2 tbsp olive oil
175 g/6 oz crabmeat
4 hard-boiled eggs
4 tbsp chopped parsley

■ Cook the pasta in boiling salted water for 3 minutes. Drain well and place in a bowl. Trim and coarsely grate the courgettes, then add them to the pasta with the spring onions. Use scissors to shred the basil and soft stalk ends into the salad. Sprinkle in seasoning to taste and mix in the lemon juice. Add the olive oil and mix well. Arrange the mixture in a serving dish, leaving a hollow in the middle.
■ Flake the crabmeat. Chop the eggs and mix them with the crab. Fork in the parsley and seasoning to taste, then spoon the mixture into the middle of the pasta. Serve at once; if the salad is allowed to stand, the pasta and courgettes become watery.

PECAN-ENCRUSTED FLOUNDER

CUBA

If you don't wish to finish this crunchy delight with a butter sauce, skip that step and douse it with garlicky aioli.

SERVES 4

salt and freshly ground
  pepper, to taste
8 small flounder fillets,
  about 225 g/8 oz total,
  skinned
1 large egg
3 tbsp water
2 tsp dark soy sauce
75 g/3 oz pecans, finely
  chopped

3 tbsp vegetable oil
2 tbsp olive oil (optional)
3 tbsp chopped fresh
  coriander or parsley for
  garnish (optional)
2 tbsp butter or margarine
  (optional)
1 tbsp freshly squeezed
  lime juice (optional)

■ Salt and pepper both sides of fillets. Whisk the egg, water and soy sauce together in a large bowl. Dip the fillets, one at a time, in the egg mixture to coat lightly, then dredge evenly in nuts. In a large nonstick frying pan over medium-high heat, heat 1 tablespoon of the vegetable oil. When hot, add as many fillets as will fit without crowding. Sauté for about 2 minutes, or until lightly browned on both sides. Add more oil, if needed. Garnish and serve the fillets.

■ If you wish to serve the fish with a butter sauce, transfer the fillets to a warm serving plate and wipe frying pan with kitchen paper. Add the remaining olive oil and butter or margarine. Heat until the butter foams and starts to brown. Add the lime juice, stir once and then pour the mixture over the fish. Garnish and serve.

CRAB-STUFFED FISH

BARBADOS

Use whole trout, red snapper, red mullet, plaice or sole for this dish, cooked individually if you use small fish. Alternatively, present an elegant platter of a large, stuffed fish surrounded by lemon slices and parsley sprigs. Fresh crabmeat is best for the stuffing, but frozen or canned are acceptable.

SERVES 4

25 g/1 oz butter
6 spring onions, chopped
125 g/4 oz coarsely
  chopped mushrooms
1 tbsp chopped fresh
  parsley
1 garlic clove, finely
  chopped
¼ tsp salt
¼ tsp paprika
¼ tsp black pepper
2 tbsp grated Parmesan
  cheese
50 ml/2 fl oz double or
  single cream

225 g/8 oz fresh
  crabmeat, picked over
4 whole fish, about
  225 g/8 oz each, or 1
  large fish about 1.25–
  1.5 kg/2½–3 lb,
  cleaned and boned
salt and freshly ground
  black pepper, to taste
flour for dredging
  (optional)
olive oil or melted butter

■ In a small frying pan, melt the butter. Sauté the onions, mushrooms, parsley and garlic until limp, about 5 minutes. Stir in the salt, paprika, pepper, Parmesan and cream until well mixed. Add the crab, stirring gently. Set aside.

■ Rinse the fish and pat dry with kitchen paper. Season the insides lightly with salt and pepper. You may dredge the trout in flour at this point, thinly coating the outside only and shaking off excess. The flouring step is optional. Preheat the oven to 180°C/350°F/Gas Mark 4.

■ Stuff the fish with the crab mixture, then skewer them closed with cocktail sticks, or sew a few large stitches with coarse thread. Put the fish in a lightly oiled baking tin and brush with olive oil or drizzle with melted butter. Bake until the flesh at thickest point is opaque but still juicy, about 10 minutes. Do not wait for the fish to flake easily because it continues cooking after it is removed from the oven, and would be overcooked by the time you serve it.

SWORDFISH WITH SAFFRON

ITALY

*Any firm white fish – halibut, monkfish or cod – is good cooked like this.
New potatoes and spinach or a salad are suitable accompaniments.*

SERVES 4

700 g/1½ lb swordfish
  steak, cut in chunks
4 tbsp sunflower oil plus
  extra for cooking
2 tbsp lemon juice
225 ml/8 fl oz dry white
  wine
1 bay leaf
1 thyme sprig

salt and freshly ground
  black pepper
1 tsp saffron strands
4 tbsp plain flour
2 leeks, thinly sliced
2 carrots, cut into
  matchstick strips
2 celery sticks, thinly sliced
225 ml/8 fl oz single cream

■ Place the fish in a dish. In a jar with a tight-fitting lid, combine half the oil, the lemon juice, wine, bay leaf, thyme and seasoning. Shake the mixture until the oil is thoroughly combined, then pour it over the fish. Cover and leave to marinate for several hours.

■ Pound the saffron strands to a powder, then stir in 2 tablespoons boiling water. Stir until the saffron has dissolved completely and set aside.

■ Drain the fish, reserving the marinade, then mop the cubes on kitchen paper. Toss them in the flour, adding a little seasoning. Heat the remaining oil and stir-fry the fish until golden brown. Use a slotted spoon to transfer the fish to a serving dish or individual plates and keep hot. Add a little extra oil and stir-fry the leeks, carrots and celery over high heat for 2 to 3 minutes, until they are lightly cooked.

■ Arrange the vegetables alongside the fish, then pour the reserved marinade into the pan and bring to the boil. Boil hard until reduced by half, then reduce the heat and stir in the cream. Add the saffron liquid and heat gently to warm the cream. Do not boil. Spoon the sauce over or around the fish and serve at once.

LEMON-SCENTED POMPANO ON SPINACH AND LEEKS

CUBA

Pompano, a renowned Florida fish, is worth some pomp and circumstance.
Considered a delicacy even in Florida, it may be hard to find.
Substitute any firm-fleshed, thin white fish or sea scallops.

SERVES 4

1 small lemon, thinly sliced
1 small lime, thinly sliced
6 bay leaves
375 ml/12 fl oz water
1 large leek, split, thinly
   sliced crosswise and
   rinsed
450 g/1 lb spinach or
   Swiss chard, stems
   removed

225 g/8 oz pompano
   fillets or substitute (see
   above)
1 tsp mild soy sauce
freshly ground black
   pepper

▇ In a steamer, combine the lemon, lime, bay leaves and water. Combine and simmer over low heat 2 minutes. Bring liquid to a boil over high heat. Spread sliced leeks one layer thick in steamer basket. Cover and steam until tender, about 3 minutes. Uncover, pack in all the spinach, cover and steam, stirring once, until wilted, about 4 minutes. Transfer steamer basket to the sink and press spinach-leek mixture very lightly to extract excess moisture.

▇ Transfer spinach-leek mixture to a large frying pan and set aside. Return water with lemon, lime and bay leaves to a boil over high heat. Lay the fish fillets in steamer basket, cover and steam until the fish are just cooked through and flake easily if tested with tip of knife, 3 to 4 minutes. Quickly reheat spinach over high heat, sprinkling soya sauce on top and tossing, about 1 minute.

▇ To serve, arrange spinach and fish on warm plates. Season fish with pepper to taste.

SQUID **P**ROVENÇAL

FRANCE

SERVES 4

8 medium squid
4 tbsp plain flour
salt and freshly ground
  black pepper
6 tbsp olive oil
1 onion, halved and sliced
1 green pepper, thinly
  sliced

1–2 garlic cloves, crushed
1 bay leaf
450 g/1 lb ripe tomatoes,
  peeled and quartered
50 g/2 oz stoned black
  olives, sliced
4 tbsp chopped fresh
  parsley

■ First clean the squid. Slice the body sac into rings and cut up the tentacles, if using, into small pieces. Dry the prepared squid on kitchen paper, then place the pieces in a basin.

■ Sprinkle the flour and plenty of seasoning over the squid. Heat the oil and stir-fry the squid briskly until lightly browned. Use a slotted spoon to remove the pieces from the pan and drain them on kitchen paper.

■ Add the onion, pepper, garlic and bay leaf to the oil remaining in the pan. Stir-fry these ingredients until the onion and pepper are slightly softened – about 5 minutes. Add the tomatoes and continue cooking, stirring all the time, for a further 5 minutes, until the tomatoes are soft but not pulpy. Add seasoning to taste and the olives, then replace the squid in the pan. Sprinkle in the parsley and stir over high heat for a minute or so. Serve with rice or plenty of crusty bread.

SKATE WITH **P**EAS AND **P**OTATOES IN **P**APRIKA **S**AUCE

SPAIN

With a red sauce and green peas, this is a colourful recipe for every type of white fish. It is often garnished with strips of cooked red pepper, which enhance the colouring.

SERVES 4

4 portions of skate wing
  (or monkfish)
salt and freshly ground
  black pepper
about 2 tsp paprika
450 g/1 lb small potatoes,
  sliced
4 small onions, sliced in
  rings
1 tbsp chopped oregano

1 bay leaf
275 g/9 oz fresh or
  frozen peas
4 tbsp olive oil
4 garlic cloves, sliced in
  rounds
1 tbsp white wine vinegar
2 canned pimentos or
  strips of cooked red
  pepper (optional)

■ Season the pieces of fish with salt, pepper and 1 teaspoon of paprika and set aside while you prepare the potatoes.

■ Place the potato slices in the base of a wide flameproof casserole, cover with the onions, sprinkle with oregano and add the bay leaf. Add water just to cover and put over a high heat. Simmer for 15 minutes.

■ Add the peas and lay the fish pieces over the top. Turn down the heat, cover and cook until the potatoes are done – about 15 minutes.

■ Drain off the liquid and measure 125 ml/4 fl oz of stock. Heat the oil in a small saucepan with the garlic. When it starts to colour, remove the pan from the heat and add the fish stock, vinegar and the remaining teaspoon of paprika. Bring to simmering and pour over the casserole contents. Garnish, if you like, with strips of red pepper. Allow the casserole to stand in a warm oven (or over very low heat) for about 5 to 10 minutes to let the flavours blend together.

SPICY SHARK KEBABS

UNITED STATES

SERVES 4

2 garlic cloves, crushed
125 ml/4 fl oz olive oil
700 g/1½ lb shark or
  swordfish steak, cut into
  kebab-sized cubes
2 tbsp fresh lime juice
1 small aubergine, cubed
1 courgette, cut into
  1-cm/½-in slices

16 medium mushrooms
1 onion, cut into chunks
1 green or red pepper, cut
  into chunks
2 tbsp ground cumin
2 tbsp paprika
1 tsp cayenne pepper
2 tsp freshly ground black
  pepper

■ If you are using wooden skewers, soak them in water for at least 30 minutes so they don't catch fire. Ignite barbecue coals about 30 minutes before you want to begin grilling.

■ Mix the garlic with 50 ml/2 fl oz olive oil and set aside to steep. Alternatively put the oil and garlic into a small bowl and microwave on Medium/50% power for 4 to 5 minutes, until garlic sizzles and is lightly browned. Set aside.

■ Put the fish into a glass or ceramic bowl. Mix remaining olive oil with lime juice and pour it over the fish. Toss well and leave to marinate about 20 minutes.

■ While fish is marinating prepare the vegetables. Place the aubergine, courgette and mushrooms in a glass or ceramic bowl. Discard the garlic from the olive oil and pour the oil over the vegetables. Toss quickly to spread the oil evenly, since the vegetables soak up liquid like sponges.

■ Drain the fish. Combine the cumin, paprika, cayenne and pepper. Then sprinkle about two-thirds of the spice mixture over the fish and toss well. Sprinkle the remaining spice mix over the vegetables and toss.

■ Thread the fish, seasoned vegetables, onion and pepper on to skewers. Do not press the pieces too tightly together, as they will not cook evenly. Lightly oil the barbecue grill. When the coals are white and no longer flaming, place the skewers on the grill over the coals. Turn once or twice, until fish is flaky and loses its translucency – about 10 minutes for every 2.5 cm/1 in of the fish's thickness.

FISH IN **H**ORSERADISH **S**AUCE

POLAND

This simple dish of cod in a creamy horseradish sauce is quite delicious.

SERVES 4

450 g/1 lb cod fillet, skinned and cut into four portions
2 bay leaves
salt and freshly ground black pepper
225 ml/8 fl oz water
25 g/1 oz butter

25 g/1 oz plain flour
3 tbsp grated horseradish
300 ml/½ pt soured cream

GARNISH
dill or parsley sprigs
lemon slices

■ Place the fish in a shallow pan and add the bay leaves. Sprinkle with seasoning, pour in the water and heat gently until simmering. Cook gently for 3 to 5 minutes, until the fish is just cooked. Use a fish slice to transfer the pieces of fish to an ovenproof dish. Strain the fish cooking liquor and reserve.

■ Set the oven at 220°C/425°F/Gas Mark 7. Melt the butter in a small saucepan and stir in the flour. Gradually pour the reserved fish cooking liquor on to the flour mixture, stirring all the time. Add the horseradish and bring to the boil to make a very thick sauce. Stir in a little seasoning and the soured cream. Spoon the sauce over the fish.
■ Bake for about 10 minutes, until the sauce is just beginning to brown. Garnish with dill and lemon, then serve at once.

RUB-A-DUB **F**ISH **F**RY

PUERTO RICO

The practice of rubbing food with escharqui *(seasonings) dates back to Ancient Peru. The technique eventually spread to the Caribbean Islands, where its name was corrupted to 'jerky', and a culinary art form grew up around it. Jerks are made in liquid, paste and dry forms, but all impart spiciness and tenderness to the food. This traditional jerk recipe from Baja uses flying fish, but fillets of any white, firm-fleshed fish may be substituted – for example red snapper, perch, turbot or sole.*

SERVES 4–6

6 flying fish or any white fish fillets
1 small onion, finely chopped
salt
white pepper
dash of Angostura bitters
1 garlic clove, finely crushed

sprig of fresh thyme, finely chopped
sprig of fresh marjoram, finely chopped
vegetable oil
1 tbsp dark rum
1 egg
breadcrumbs

■ Rinse the fish fillets and dry with kitchen paper. Combine the onion, salt, white pepper, bitters, garlic, thyme and marjoram. Rub the mixture firmly into the fillets on both sides.
■ In a frying pan large enough to hold all the fillets (or use two frying pans), heat the oil to medium-hot. Beat the rum and egg together. Dip each fillet into the egg, then coat with breadcrumbs. Fry for 2 to 3 minutes on each side until the fish is opaque.

STEAMED FISH CURRY

THAILAND

SERVES 6–8

325 g/11 oz fish fillets (flounder, sole or sea bass), skinned and cut into slices

600 ml/1 pt thin coconut milk

2 eggs, beaten

3 tbsp fish sauce

60 g/2½ oz sweet basil leaves

75 g/3 oz finely sliced cabbage

6 squares of banana leaf (optional)

1½ tbsp cornflour

2 kaffir lime leaves, torn into small pieces

1 fresh red chilli, seeded and cut into strips

RED CURRY PASTE

10 small garlic cloves, chopped lightly

5 dried red chillies, chopped lightly

5 white peppercorns

3 shallots, chopped lightly

2 coriander roots, sliced

1 tsp sliced galangal

1 tsp chopped lemon grass

½ tsp finely chopped kaffir lime zest

½ tsp salt

■ Pound all the ingredients for the paste together with a mortar and pestle or in a blender until fine. Put in a bowl and stir in the fish pieces and 450 ml/¾ pt of the coconut milk. Break in the eggs, then stir in the fish sauce.

■ Divide the basil and cabbage between the banana leaf squares or 6 to 8 ovenproof ramekins. Top with the fish mixture and wrap up. Cook in a pressure cooker, or bake in a 180°C/350°F/Gas Mark 4 oven, covered, in a pan half-filled with hot water, for 10 minutes.

■ Meanwhile, boil the remaining 150 ml/¼ pt of coconut milk in a pan, and add the cornflour to thicken slightly.

■ After the fish mixture has cooked for 10 minutes, spoon the thickened coconut milk over the tops and sprinkle with the lime leaf and chilli. Pressure-cook or bake again for 5 more minutes. Stand for 5 minutes before serving with rice.

YEREVAN-STYLE TROUT

RUSSIA

The trout from Sevan Lake is said to be the most delicious in Russia. This recipe combines the flavours of that region, though we cannot duplicate the unique lake fish.

SERVES 4

4 brown or rainbow trout, 350 g/12 oz each, cleaned and gutted

salt and freshly ground black pepper

50 g/2 oz unsalted butter

225 g/8 oz bottled artichoke hearts in oil

50 g/2 oz plain flour

150 ml/¼ pt fresh lemon juice

225 ml/8 fl oz water

75 ml/3 fl oz vegetable oil

1½ tbsp dry white wine

3 tbsp drained capers

3 tbsp finely chopped fresh flat-leaved parsley

pinch of sweet paprika

small pinch of cayenne pepper

■ Rinse the trout and pat it dry with kitchen paper. Season to taste and set aside.

■ In a heavy saucepan over low heat, gently melt the butter until the solids have sunk to the bottom of the pan. Slowly pour off the clarified butter on the top and set aside. Discard the white residue and wash the pan.

■ Pour the oil from the bottled artichokes into the saucepan. Add 1 teaspoon flour and heat over a medium flame, stirring. Slowly add half the lemon juice and the water and bring the liquid to the boil, whisking. Lower the heat to simmer, stir in the artichoke hearts and cook, uncovered, for about 10 minutes, or until the sauce is reduced and thickened. Set aside.

■ Preheat the oven to 190°C/375°F/Gas Mark 5. Dredge the trout in the remaining flour and shake off the excess. Heat half the oil in a frying pan and brown two of the trout on one side only. Remove to a roasting tin lined with oiled foil, add the rest of the oil to the frying pan and brown the two remaining trout on one side. Transfer to the roasting tin. Bake the trout for 10 minutes, or until the flesh is opaque and just beginning to flake. Carefully fillet the trout, arrange on four warmed serving plates and sprinkle with the wine.

■ Stir the remaining lemon juice, the clarified butter and the capers into the sauce and heat through. Spoon the mixture over the fillets and sprinkle with the chopped parsley and the spices. Serve immediately.

SALT COD WITH ONIONS AND POTATOES

PORTUGAL

*This dish, one of the most famous salt cod dishes, comes from Porto,
and is named after a restaurateur, Gomes de Sá,
who is reputed to have been its creator.*

SERVES 4

450 g/1 lb salt cod, well
  soaked
700 g/1½ lb even-sized
  potatoes, unpeeled
1 Spanish onion, sliced
  thinly into rings
3 tbsp olive oil
16 oil-cured olives, stoned
large bunch of chopped
  parsley leaves (about
  25 g/1 oz)

freshly ground black
  pepper
2 hard-boiled eggs, shelled
  and quartered
chopped parsley and
  stoned black olives, to
  garnish
lemon wedges, to serve

■ Put the cod into a saucepan, cover with water and simmer for 15 minutes. Drain and leave until cool. Remove and discard any skin and bones. Flake the flesh using two forks.

■ Boil the potatoes until tender. Drain and leave until cool enough to handle; then peel and slice thinly. Meanwhile, cook the onion in the oil until softened. Preheat the oven to 180°C/350°F/Gas Mark 4.

■ Layer the potatoes, onion and fish in a well-oiled baking dish, sprinkling each layer with the olives, parsley and pepper. Finish with a layer of onion rings. Bake for 35 to 40 minutes until lightly browned.

■ Arrange the quartered eggs on top and garnish with parsley and black olives. Serve with lemon wedges.

SEAFOOD MEDLEY

ITALY

You can vary the mixture of seafood according to your budget, the choice at the fishmongers and personal preference. Remember to add delicate ingredients at the end so they do not overcook. Serve with plain pasta or try combining a mixture of tomato, spinach and plain pasta.

SERVES 4

900 g/2 lb mussels
1 bay leaf
300 ml/½ pt dry white wine
6 tbsp olive oil
1 onion, halved and thinly sliced
1 celery stick, finely diced
1 green pepper, seeded and finely diced
3 garlic cloves, crushed
grated rind of 1 lemon
salt and freshly ground black pepper

4 small squid, cleaned and sliced
350 g/12 oz monkfish fillet, cut in small chunks
6–8 scallops, shelled and sliced
350 g/12 oz peeled cooked prawns, thawed if frozen
8 black olives, stoned and chopped
plenty of chopped parsley
freshly grated Parmesan cheese, to serve

■ Scrub the mussels and scrape off any barnacles or dirt on the shell. Pull away the black beard which protrudes from the shell. Discard any open mussels which do not shut when tapped. Place the mussels in a large pan and add the bay leaf and wine. Bring the wine to the boil, then put a close-fitting lid on the pan and reduce the heat slightly so that the mussels don't boil too rapidly. Cook for about 10 minutes, shaking the pan often, until all the mussels are open. Discard any that are shut. Strain the mussels, reserving the cooking liquor and bay leaf. Use a fork to remove the mussels from their shells.

■ Heat the oil in a large saucepan. Add the reserved bay leaf, onion, celery, green pepper, garlic, lemon rind and plenty of seasoning. Cover and cook, stirring occasionally, for 20 minutes, or until the onion is softened but not browned. Pour in the reserved cooking liquor, bring to a boil and boil hard for about 3 minutes, or until reduced by half. Then reduce the heat and add the squid. Cover the pan and simmer for 5 minutes. Add the monkfish, cover the pan again and cook for a further 5 minutes. Next, add the scallops and cook gently for 3 minutes.

■ Add the prawns, mussels and olives. Heat gently, then taste for seasoning. Stir in plenty of parsley and serve at once, with Parmesan cheese.

PRAWNS FRIED WITH GARLIC AND PEPPER

THAILAND

SERVES 4

approx. 125 ml/4 fl oz peanut or corn oil for frying
325 g/11 oz raw prawns, shelled

½ tbsp lightly chopped garlic
2 tbsp ground white pepper
1 tsp salt

■ Heat the oil in a pan or wok, add the prawns and brown lightly for about 2 minutes. Remove all but a quarter of the oil and add the garlic, pepper and salt to the pan. Fry lightly for 2 more minutes until brown. Drain off most of the remaining oil and serve immediately with rice and sliced cucumber.

BISCAY BAY SOLE WITH CREAM AND SHELLFISH

SPAIN

The superb fish we know as Dover sole in the English Channel is fished all across the Bay of Biscay, right down to the Basque coast. This type of rich, old-fashioned cooking, with a cream sauce, has been typical for a century or more. Shellfish make the perfect garnish, and done this way they provide the stock for the dish.

SERVES 4

2 tbsp chopped onion
6 black peppercorns
4 tbsp chopped fresh parsley
1 bay leaf
200 ml/7 fl oz dry white wine
16 medium-size clams or mussels, cleaned
4 tbsp butter
4 Dover sole or plaice fillets
about 1½ tbsp flour
salt and ground white pepper
125 ml/4 fl oz whipping cream

▪ Put the chopped onion in a saucepan with the peppercorns, 2 tablespoons of parsley, the bay leaf and the wine. Bring to a simmer. Put in the clams or mussels, cover and cook for 1 to 2 minutes until they open. Remove the shellfish, then let the liquid boil for 5 minutes and reserve. Take one shell off each mussel (discarding any that are still shut).

▪ Melt the butter in a frying pan. Dust the fish fillets in seasoned flour and fry (probably two at a time) for a couple of minutes on each side. Remove to a serving plate and keep warm.

▪ Add 1 teaspoon of flour to the pan and stir into the butter. Strain in the reserved shellfish stock, add the cream and stir to deglaze the pan. Boil to reduce the sauce by half, adding the shellfish, face upwards, to warm them. This sauce should need no seasoning, but taste to check. Pour over the sole, sprinkle with parsley and serve. Slim leeks make good partners for this dish.

SEAFOOD GUMBO WITH OKRA

UNITED STATES

Okra is used as the thickener, so this gumbo is lighter than a roux-based gumbo. It is only mildly spicy. Use at least three different types of fish and shellfish, in whatever combination of fresh seafood is available: prawns, crab, oysters, frogs' legs, crayfish tails, clams, mussels, scallops, or filleted redfish, red snapper, cod or other fish, cut into cubes.

SERVES 8

2 tbsp vegetable oil
450 g/1 lb onions, chopped
2 large green peppers, chopped
2 celery stalks, chopped
3 garlic cloves, finely chopped
3 large or 4 medium tomatoes, seeded and chopped
225-g/8-oz can tomato sauce
1.75 ltr/3 pt fish stock
1 tbsp freshly squeezed lemon juice
2 bay leaves
1 tbsp fresh thyme or 1 tsp dried
1 tsp salt
¼ tsp black pepper
large pinch cayenne pepper
large pinch white pepper
½ tsp paprika
700 g/1½ lb okra, thawed and well drained if frozen, sliced
900 g/2 lb mixed seafood
450 g/1 lb cooked rice to serve
filé powder (optional)

▪ In a large frying pan, heat the oil. Sauté the onion, pepper, celery and garlic until limp, about 5 minutes. Transfer to a large saucepan or stockpot and add the tomatoes, tomato sauce, fish stock, lemon juice and seasonings. Bring to the boil, then reduce the heat and simmer, uncovered, 5 minutes.

▪ Add the okra and return to the boil, then reduce the heat and simmer 30 minutes. Add the seafood: cubed fish and frogs' legs take the longest times to cook, oysters the least.

▪ Spoon the rice into individual large bowls. Ladle the gumbo over the rice. If desired, add a pinch of filé powder to each bowl.

CASEROLED PRAWNS WITH GLASS NOODLES

THAILAND

*The size of the prawns is unimportant; you could also use
lobster tails or crab claws.*

SERVES 6

2 bacon rashers, cut into
2.5-cm/1-in pieces
6 prawns, shelled
2 coriander roots, cut in
half
25 g/1 oz root ginger,
pounded or chopped
finely
25 g/1 oz garlic,
chopped
1 tbsp white peppercorns,
crushed
450 g/1 lb cellophane
noodles, soaked in cold
water for 10 minutes

1 tsp butter
3 tbsp black soy sauce
10 g/¼ oz roughly
chopped coriander
leaves and stems

SOUP STOCK
450 ml/¾ pt chicken stock
2 tbsp oyster sauce
2 tbsp black soy sauce
½ tbsp sesame seed oil
1 tsp brandy or whisky
½ tsp sugar

■ Place all the soup stock ingredients in a pan, bring
to a boil and simmer for 5 minutes. Leave to cool.
■ Take a heatproof casserole dish or heavy-bottomed
pan and place the bacon over the base. Put in the
prawns, coriander root, ginger, garlic and peppercorns.
Place the noodles over the top, then add the butter, soy
sauce and soup stock.
■ Place on the heat, cover, bring to a boil and simmer
for 5 minutes. Mix well with tongs, add the chopped
coriander, cover and cook again until the prawns are
cooked, about 5 minutes more. Remove excess stock
liquid before serving.

RED SNAPPER, YUCATAN STYLE

MEXICO

*If you are unable to find red snapper, try this dish with sole,
sea bass or sea bream instead.*

SERVES 4

2 small peppers, one red,
  one green, seeded and
  chopped
1 medium onion, chopped
2 garlic cloves, finely
  chopped
50 g/2 oz butter
2 tbsp chopped coriander
  leaves
1 tsp whole cumin

½ tsp grated orange rind
salt and pepper to taste
125 ml/4 fl oz freshly
  squeezed orange juice
1 red snapper, 2 kg/
  4½ lb, cleaned and
  scaled
6–8 sliced black olives
1 large or 2 small
  avocados, for garnish

■ Fry the peppers, onion and garlic in 25 g/1 oz butter, until softened. Add the coriander, cumin, orange rind and orange juice; season to taste. Simmer for 2 minutes. Preheat the oven to 180°C/350°F/Gas Mark 4.

■ Thickly grease the bottom of a large, shallow casserole with the remaining butter. Put the fish in the casserole and cover it with the pepper mixture. Scatter the olives over the top. Bake for about 30 minutes, basting occasionally with the sauce. Serve hot, garnished with thin slices of avocado.

FISH AND VEGETABLE CASSEROLE

GREECE

Cod, haddock or monkfish would all be suitable types of fish to use for this dish, which originates from the Greek island of Corfu. The crucial ingredient is the garlic, and plenty of it.

SERVES 8–10

75 ml/3 fl oz olive oil
1 large onion, sliced
900 g/2 lb small new potatoes, washed and cut into 1.5-cm/1-in rounds
2 carrots, cut into 2.5-cm/1-in chunks
1 celery stick, chopped

salt and freshly ground black pepper, to taste
6 garlic cloves, crushed
1.25 kg/2½ lb firm white fish fillets, skinned and cut into 5-cm/2-in chunks
50 ml/2 fl oz freshly squeezed lemon juice

■ Heat 50 ml/2 fl oz of the olive oil in a large, heavy-based saucepan and sauté the onion for about 3 minutes, or until softened. Add the potatoes, carrots and celery, and season with salt and freshly ground black pepper. Continue to cook for a further 4 to 5 minutes, or until the vegetables begin to soften.

■ Stir in the garlic and pour over enough boiling water to just cover the vegetables. Bring to the boil, cover and simmer for 10 to 15 minutes, or until the vegetables are almost tender.

■ Gently stir the fish into the casserole, cover and simmer for 10 to 15 minutes, or until the fish flakes easily, adding a little extra water if necessary. Just before the end of the cooking time, remove the cover and stir in the lemon juice and the remaining olive oil. Adjust the seasoning if necessary and serve.

TYREAN CLAMS OR MUSSELS

LEBANON

Tyre was renowned in ancient times for its purple dye, reserved for Roman aristocrats and derived from the crushed shells of whelks. But that was not the only shellfish that thrived on the sea-shelf fronting the harbour: mussels, several types of clam, prawns and crayfish graced the Tyrean table and were transported inland. The tradition remains.

SERVES 4–6

1 garlic clove, crushed
1 small red onion, thinly sliced
225 ml/8 fl oz white wine
900 g/2 lb prairie clams or small mussels

4 plum tomatoes, peeled, seeded and chopped
2 tbsp lemon juice
1 tbsp butter
1 tbsp finely chopped fresh coriander

■ Put the garlic and chopped onion into the wine in a deep saucepan. Bring to the boil, simmer for 2 minutes, then add the mussels or clams. Bring back to the boil, lower the heat and simmer, covered, for about 5 minutes, or until the shellfish open. Discard any mussels or clams that have not opened.

■ Remove the shellfish to a serving bowl and keep them warm. Add the tomatoes to the cooking liquid and mash them into it. Bring it back to the boil and reduce slightly. Just before serving, stir in the lemon juice, butter and coriander. Pour over the clams or mussels and serve immediately with pitta bread to mop up the sauce.

POACHED **S**ALMON **F**ILLETS WITH **D**ILL-AND-GINGER **V**INAIGRETTE

—— PUERTO RICO ——

SERVES 4

4 boneless salmon fillets,
   175 g/6 oz each, with
   skin on
9 large sprigs fresh dill
1 bay leaf
4 whole cloves
salt
9 whole black peppercorns
2 tbsp white wine vinegar

DILL-AND-GINGER
VINAIGRETTE
2 tbsp French mustard
1 tbsp grated root ginger
2 tbsp finely chopped
   shallot
1 tsp finely chopped garlic
2 tbsp tarragon vinegar
50 g/2 oz canned
   pimentos, diced
salt and freshly ground
   black pepper
125 ml/4 fl oz olive oil

■ Prepare the vinaigrette by whisking the mustard, ginger, shallot, garlic, vinegar, pimentos and salt and pepper together in a bowl. Then add the olive oil in a slow stream, whisking rapidly until well blended. Set aside.

■ Place the salmon fillets in a shallow saucepan with enough water to cover. Add all but one dill sprig, the bay leaf, cloves, salt, peppercorns and vinegar. Bring the water to the boil and simmer for 3 to 5 minutes. Do not overcook. Drain and serve with the vinaigrette, giving the vinaigrette a last-second whisking, if necessary. Float the reserved sprig of dill on top of the bowl of vinaigrette.

CURRIED FISH FILLETS

INDIA

*This dish comes from the southern city of Cochin, one of the Jewish communities
in India. Cochin is near the Kerala coast, which produces fresh fish
and is also famous for its spice market. This is best served with rice.*

SERVES 6

1 tbsp vegetable oil
1 onion, cut in half and
  thinly sliced
2–3 garlic cloves, peeled
  and finely chopped
900 g/2 lb white fish
  fillets, such as cod,
  halibut or whiting, cut in
  7.5-cm/3-in pieces
40 g/1½ oz fresh
  coriander leaves,
  chopped

1 tbsp white or red wine
  vinegar
4 tbsp tomato purée
1 tsp ground cumin
½ tsp turmeric
1 small fresh red chilli, or
  ½ tsp red pepper flakes
fresh coriander sprigs for
  garnish

■ In a large frying pan, over medium-high heat, heat oil. Add sliced onion and cook until softened and beginning to colour, 3 to 5 minutes. Add garlic and cook 1 minute longer.

■ Add the fish fillets and cook until they begin to firm and turn opaque, 4 to 5 minutes. Gently stir in remaining ingredients, except garnish, and 125 ml/ 4 fl oz water; simmer 15 minutes, covered. The fish will flake easily if tested with the tip of a knife.

■ Transfer the fish to a serving dish. Increase heat to high and cook sauce until slightly thickened, 2 to 3 minutes. Pour over fish. Garnish with coriander sprigs and serve with hot rice.

ACKEE AND SALT FISH

— JAMAICA —

SERVES 6

900 g/2 lb salt cod
50 ml/2 fl oz vegetable oil
1 onion, sliced
1 garlic clove, crushed
1 fresh hot pepper,
  chopped

2 tomatoes, skinned and
  chopped
400-g/14-oz can ackee

■ Soak the cod overnight to remove the salt. Next day, drain it, then rinse it well under cold running water and break into flakes. Discard the skin and bones. Heat the oil in a frying pan, add the onion, garlic and hot pepper and fry over a low heat until they are soft.

■ Add the prepared salt cod and fry for 5 minutes, stirring constantly. Add the tomatoes and cook for 5 more minutes. Add the ackee and cook until it looks like scrambled eggs.

■ Serve hot with rice 'n' peas and fried plantains.

SPICY SEAFOOD SALAD

THAILAND

Thai versions of salad are flavourful assemblies of ingredients, quite unlikely those we are accustomed to in the West. Most are extremely spicy. This salad combines three of the basic five flavours: spicy, sour and salty.

SERVES 6

150 g/5 oz sea bass or perch, cleaned, gutted and sliced thinly into strips
150 g/5 oz prawns, shelled
150 g/5 oz squid, cleaned, gutted and sliced into 2-cm/¾-in strips
7 fresh small green chillies

5 garlic cloves
2 coriander roots
2 tbsp Nuoc Mam sauce
½ tsp sugar
2 tbsp lime or lemon juice
4 spring onions, sliced into 5-mm/¼-in pieces
125 g/4 oz onions, sliced thinly
50 g/2 oz celery leaves and stems, sliced

■ Cook the fish, prawns and squid separately in salted water until cooked, about 2 to 3 minutes each, and drain.

■ Pound the chillies, garlic, coriander root, Nuoc Mam sauce and sugar together with a pestle and mortar or in a blender until fine. Place in a bowl and mix in the lemon juice, spring onions, onion and celery. Stir in the fish and seafood and mix well. Serve immediately.

VEGETARIAN

ASPARAGUS SUPREME

ITALY

This is really simple and quite unbeatable, especially if you are able to raid a pick-your-own farm for the freshest possible asparagus and cook the vegetable while it still spits with zest as you snap the spears. If you are having a healthy spell, toss the asparagus in 1 tablespoon hot olive oil and mix some fromage frais into the pasta instead of using lots and lots of butter!

SERVES 4

450 g/1 lb asparagus,
  trimmed of woody ends
  if necessary
450 g/1 lb tagliatelle
  verdi or spinach-
  flavoured small pasta
  shapes

75 g/3 oz butter
salt and freshly ground
  black pepper
3 tbsp chopped fresh dill
freshly grated Parmesan
  cheese, to serve
  (optional)

■ Tie the asparagus in a bundle, stand upright in a pan of boiling salted water and cook for 10 to 20 minutes, until just tender. If you do not have a tall asparagus saucepan, use the deepest pan you have, stand the asparagus in it and tent foil over the top of the pan, crumpling it securely around the rim to seal in the steam. Very fresh, young asparagus will cook in 10 minutes, larger or more mature spears take longer.

■ Cook the pasta in another large pan of boiling salted water. Meanwhile, heat the butter in a medium pan. Drain the asparagus and cut the spears into short lengths, then add them to the butter. Add a little seasoning, then pour the asparagus mixture over the drained pasta. Sprinkle with dill and mix well. Serve at once, with freshly grated Parmesan if you like.

CAULIFLOWER BAKED WITH TOMATOES AND FETA

GREECE

This dish is enlivened with a strong flavour of tomatoes combined with the typically Greek use of ground cinnamon to give that extra special taste.

SERVES 4–6

75 ml/3 fl oz olive oil
1 onion, sliced
2 garlic cloves, crushed
8 tomatoes, seeded and chopped
large pinch of ground cinnamon
2 tsp dried oregano

salt and freshly ground black pepper, to taste
1 large cauliflower, cut into florets
1 tbsp freshly squeezed lemon juice
75 g/3 oz feta cheese, crumbled

■ Heat 2 to 3 tablespoons olive oil in a heavy-based frying pan and sauté the onion and garlic for 3 to 4 minutes, or until the onion has softened.

■ Add the tomatoes, cinnamon and oregano and season with salt and pepper. Stir and simmer, covered, for 5 minutes.

■ Preheat the oven to 190°C/375°F/Gas Mark 5. Add the cauliflower to the tomato mixture, cover and simmer for a further 10 to 15 minutes, or until the cauliflower is just tender. Remove from the heat.

■ Transfer the cauliflower and tomato mixture to a large, shallow dish and drizzle over the remaining olive oil. Sprinkle over the lemon juice and crumbled feta. Bake for 45 to 50 minutes, or until the cauliflower is soft and the cheese has melted. Serve warm.

SMOKED TOFU WITH PASTA

---- ITALY ----

*Pasta flavoured with herbs or tomatoes goes very
well with smoked tofu.*

SERVES 4

2 tbsp olive oil
25 g/1 oz butter
4 celery sticks, finely diced
1 green pepper, seeded
  and diced
salt and freshly ground
  black pepper
450 g/1 lb smoked tofu,
  cut into small cubes

450 g/1 lb fresh pasta
  shapes
grated rind of 1 lemon
2 spring onions, finely
  chopped
3 tbsp chopped parsley
lemon wedges, to serve

■ Heat the oil and butter in a large saucepan. Add the celery and cook, stirring, for 5 minutes. Add the green pepper, a little salt and plenty of freshly ground black pepper, stir well and cook gently for a further 10 minutes. Lightly mix the tofu into the pepper and celery, then leave to heat through for about 5 minutes.

■ Cook the pasta in a large pan of boiling salted water. Mix the lemon rind, spring onions and parsley. Toss the drained pasta with the tofu mixture and serve in individual bowls. Sprinkle with the lemon rind, spring onion and parsley mixture and serve with lemon wedges. The juice from the lemon may be squeezed over the pasta.

TOFU CHOW MEIN

──── CHINA ────

SERVES 4

4 large dried Chinese mushrooms

4 tbsp soy sauce

2 tbsp dry sherry

1 garlic clove, crushed

¼ tsp five-spice powder

225 g/8 oz tofu, cubed

2 tsp cornflour

225 g/8 oz Chinese egg noodles

3 tbsp groundnut oil

1 small carrot, cut into matchstick strips

1 yellow pepper, cut into short thin strips

6 spring onions, sliced diagonally

200-g/7-oz can water chestnuts, drained and sliced

225 g/8 oz beansprouts

■ Place the dried mushrooms in a small basin or mug and pour in just enough hot water to cover them. Use a saucer or base of a second mug to press the mushrooms down and keep them submerged. Leave to soak for 20 minutes.

■ Mix the soy sauce, sherry, garlic and five-spice powder, then pour this mixture over the tofu and set aside.

■ Drain the mushrooms, reserving the liquid. Discard their tough stalks, then slice the caps. Blend the cornflour to a paste with the soaking liquid.

■ Place the noodles in a pan and cover with boiling water. Bring to the boil and cook for 2 minutes, then drain and spread out on a heated serving dish. Cover with foil and keep hot.

■ Heat the oil. Drain any liquid from the tofu into the cornflour liquid, then stir-fry the tofu over high heat until golden all over. Take care at first not to break the pieces – once the tofu is crisp outside it is less likely to break up.

■ Add the carrot, pepper, mushrooms and spring onions, and stir-fry until the vegetables are slightly softened. Add the water chestnuts and continue to stir-fry for 2 minutes, or until hot.

■ Give the cornflour liquid a stir and pour it into the pan. Bring to the boil, stirring, and simmer for 1 minute. Add the beansprouts and cook, stirring for 1 minute, to heat them. Pour the mixture over the noodles and serve the dish at once.

RED BEANS AND RICE

──── UNITED STATES ────

Serve this flavourful, slow-cooked dish with salsa and soured cream. Extra vegetables are added near the end.

SERVES 6 – 8

450 g/1 lb dry kidney beans, picked over

3 tbsp olive oil

1 large onion, chopped

4 garlic cloves, finely chopped

3 celery stalks, chopped

1 carrot, chopped

1½ green peppers, seeded and chopped

1 tbsp salt

¼ tsp cayenne pepper

¼ tsp white pepper

¼ tsp black pepper

1 tsp dried thyme

1½ tsp ground cumin

1 tsp dry mustard

1 bay leaf

175-ml/6-oz tomato purée

125 ml/4 fl oz dry red wine

few drops Tabasco sauce

4 spring onions, chopped

sour cream, for garnish

SALSA

2 large tomatoes, seeded and chopped

4 spring onions, chopped

½ long mild chilli, such as Anaheim or poblano

1 tbsp fresh chopped parsley

1 tbsp white wine vinegar

1 tbsp olive oil

few drops Tabasco, to taste

■ In 4.5 ltr/1 gallon water, soak the beans at least 4 hours or overnight. Drain, rinse and return to the large pot with 1.25 ltr/2 pt water. Bring to the boil, then reduce the heat and simmer.

■ In a frying pan, heat the oil and sauté the onion, garlic, ⅔ of the celery, the carrot and ⅔ of the green pepper until wilted, about 5 minutes. Add the vegetables to the beans, along with the seasonings, tomato purée and wine, and continue simmering, stirring occasionally.

■ After about 30 minutes, taste the sauce, then add Tabasco to taste, and adjust the other seasonings. Cook the beans until tender, 1 to 1½ hours.

■ Meanwhile, in a bowl, combine all the salsa ingredients. Allow the flavours to blend for about 1 hour, then taste and add more Tabasco sauce if desired.

■ Just before serving, stir the remaining celery and green pepper into the bean mixture with the spring onions. Serve on a bed of rice. Top with salsa and soured cream.

MUSHROOM-STUFFED AUBERGINES

SPAIN

This is one of the few aubergine dishes that omits salting the flesh, so it is quick to prepare.

SERVES 2

2 aubergines, about
  350 g/12 oz each
2 tbsp olive oil
2 small onions, chopped
3 garlic cloves, finely
  chopped
200 g/7 oz mushrooms,
  preferably including wild
  ones, cleaned and sliced

salt and freshly ground
  black pepper
béchamel sauce (see
  page 37)
50 g/2 oz hard cheese,
  grated

■ Halve the aubergines lengthways and remove the flesh carefully so that the skin is not broken. Reserve the skins and chop the flesh finely.

■ Meanwhile, heat the oil in a frying pan and fry the onions until they colour. Add the garlic and mushrooms and cook until they soften. Add the aubergine flesh and fry until golden, stirring occasionally. Season the aubergine skins and the flesh in the pan, then stuff the skins with the fried mixture.

■ Pour a pool of béchamel sauce into a gratin dish. Arrange the stuffed vegetables on it, then dribble the remaining sauce into the aubergines. Sprinkle them with cheese, brown under a hot grill for 5 minutes and serve immediately.

SWEET POTATO AND OKRA KEBABS

LEBANON

This is a modern recipe, combining the traditional vegetables of the countryside – okra and onions – with the more recently introduced sweet potato. The method of cooking, however, is time-honoured.

SERVES 6

24 small okra
3 medium-sized sweet
  potatoes, peeled and
  each cut into 8 pieces
24 pickling onions

125 ml/4 fl oz olive oil
1 tbsp honey
salt and freshly ground
  pepper
½ tsp ground cumin

■ Trim off the stem end of the okra, being careful not to cut into the pods.

■ Bring a large saucepan of water to the boil. Drop in the sweet potato pieces and cook for 5 minutes. Add the onions and cook for 4 minutes, then add the okra and continue to cook for a further 1 minute. Drain the vegetables and plunge them into cold water to stop the cooking. Leave for a few minutes, then drain again. Peel the onions.

■ Thread the vegetables alternately on to 6 large or 12 small skewers. In a bowl, whisk together the oil, honey, salt and pepper to taste and cumin.

■ Baste the kebabs with the mixture and place them on a hot to medium-hot grill over grey-ashed coals (or alternatively under a preheated grill). Cook for 8 to 10 minutes, or until all the vegetables are tender, turning once and basting with the dressing occasionally. Serve immediately.

FRENCH BEANS AND NEW POTATOES IN PESTO

— UNITED STATES —

Although this dish takes advantage of the bounty of summer gardens, it can be made with potatoes and green beans that are available year-round, and pesto that is made in quantity during the summer and frozen in small batches.

SERVES 4

450 g/1 lb French beans, washed and trimmed

450 g/1 lb tiny new potatoes, washed and cut in half

2 tbsp pine nuts or chopped walnuts

1 garlic clove, peeled

40 g/1½ oz fresh basil leaves

75 g/3 oz Parmesan or Romano cheese, freshly grated if possible

5 tbsp olive oil

¼ tsp salt

pinch of black pepper

■ Boil the potatoes until tender, about 10 minutes. Boil the French beans until tender, 3 to 4 minutes. While the potatoes and beans are cooking, put the remaining ingredients in a food processor and process for about 10 seconds, until the basil is well chopped but the mixture is not turned into a paste.

■ Drain the potatoes and beans, toss with the pesto and serve.

SWEET POTATO AND WALNUT SOUFFLÉ

ANTIGUA

SERVES 6

4 small sweet potatoes
25 g/1 oz butter or
    margarine
2 tbsp flour
225 ml/8 fl oz milk
½ small onion, grated

¼ tsp thyme
freshly ground black
    pepper
4 eggs, separated
150 g/5 oz walnuts,
    chopped

■ Cook the sweet potatoes in boiling water until they are soft. Drain and leave them to cool. Peel, then mash them with a fork. Preheat the oven to its lowest setting.

■ In a saucepan, melt the butter or margarine, then stir in the flour. Gradually add the milk, stirring, and cook until the sauce thickens.

■ Remove the pan from the heat and add the onion, thyme and freshly ground black pepper. Beat the egg whites until they are stiff, then gently fold them into the sauce.

■ Add the walnuts and sweet potato, stirring them in gently. Beat the egg yolks and add these to the mixture. Pour into a greased soufflé dish. Bake in the preheated oven for 20 minutes, then serve immediately.

SPINACH WITH APPLES AND WALNUTS

FRANCE

SERVES 4

450 g/1 lb fresh spinach
3 tbsp olive oil
½ small onion, finely
    chopped
2 full-flavoured eating
    apples, peeled, cored
    and diced

75 g/3 oz walnut pieces,
    chopped
knob of butter (optional)
salt and freshly ground
    black pepper

■ Wash the spinach, then place it dripping wet in a large pan. Cover with a lid and cook over high heat, shaking the pan often, for about 3 minutes, or until the spinach has reduced in volume and softened. Drain well, pressing all the liquid from the spinach.

■ Heat the oil, then stir-fry the onion and apples until the onion has softened, but not browned. Stir in the nuts and continue stir-frying for about 5 minutes to roast them and bring out their flavour. Add the butter and heat it through before adding the spinach. Stir-fry the spinach for 3 minutes. Add seasoning to taste, then serve at once.

PUMPKIN WITH LEEKS

— UNITED STATES —

*Stir-frying is one of the best cooking methods for pumpkin
– the vegetable remains whole but slightly tender.*

SERVES 4

2 tbsp oil
knob of butter
1 garlic clove, crushed
  (optional)
2 leeks, sliced
2 tsp ground cinnamon

50 g/2 oz sultanas
450 g/1 lb prepared
  pumpkin flesh, cubed
salt and freshly ground
  black pepper

■ Heat the oil and butter until the butter melts, then add the garlic (if wished), leeks, cinnamon and sultanas. Stir-fry for 5 minutes until the leeks are softened.

■ Add the pumpkin and seasoning. Continue stir-frying until the cubes are tender, but not soft enough to become mushy, 7 to 10 minutes. Serve the dish at once with lots of crusty bread.

AUBERGINES IN COCONUT SAUCE

BARBADOS

SERVES 6

900 g/2 lb aubergines
1 tbsp salt
8 tbsp oil
2 onions, sliced
2 garlic cloves, crushed
6 tomatoes, skinned and
   chopped

300 ml/½ pt coconut milk
freshly ground black
   pepper
2 tbsp desiccated coconut

■ Cut the aubergines into 1-cm/½-in thick slices. Place them in a colander, sprinkling a little salt over each layer of slices, and leave, weighted down with a plate, for 20 minutes. Rinse off the bitter juices that have oozed out and dry with kitchen paper.

■ Heat 6 tablespoons oil in a large frying pan. Fry the aubergine slices for 10 minutes, turning them once during this time. Drain them on kitchen paper.

■ Preheat the oven to 180°C/350°F/Gas Mark 4. Heat the remaining oil in the same pan, add the onions and fry for 5 minutes over a medium heat. Add the garlic and tomatoes and cook for 3 minutes, stirring constantly.

■ Pour in the coconut milk and season to taste with salt and freshly ground black pepper. Layer the aubergine slices in an ovenproof dish and pour over the coconut sauce. Cover with foil and bake in the preheated oven for 30 minutes. Uncover, sprinkle the desiccated coconut over and bake for 5 more minutes.

CARROT AND POTATO HOTPOT

POLAND

SERVES 4

1 large onion, thinly sliced
75 g/3 oz butter
350 g/12 oz carrots,
   thickly sliced
700 g/1½ lb potatoes,
   peeled and cut in large
   chunks
salt and freshly ground
   black pepper

1 bay leaf
600 ml/1 pt water
25 g/1 oz fresh
   breadcrumbs
40 g/1½ oz plain flour
150 ml/¼ pt soured cream
2 tbsp chopped fresh dill

■ Cook the onion in one third of the butter for 10 minutes. Stir in the carrots and potatoes, then sprinkle in some seasoning. Add the bay leaf and pour in the water. Bring to the boil, then simmer, uncovered, for about 15 minutes, until the vegetables are tender.

■ Meanwhile, cook the breadcrumbs in half the remaining butter until golden. Set aside.

■ Drain the vegetables, reserving the liquid, and put them in a warmed serving dish. Melt the remaining butter in a saucepan and stir in the flour. Gradually add the cooking liquid and bring to the boil, stirring. Simmer for 3 minutes, add the soured cream and dill, and taste for seasoning. Pour this sauce over the vegetables and top with the crumbs. Serve at once.

FLAGEOLET BEANS WITH SPINACH

— FRANCE —

This no-fuss dish is ideal for summer days when spare time is best spent outdoors rather than slaving for hours in a hot kitchen.

SERVES 4

450 g/1 lb fresh spinach, trimmed and washed
knob of butter
2 tbsp olive oil
6 spring onions, chopped
2 x 425-g/15-oz cans flageolet beans, drained
2 small courgettes, trimmed and thinly sliced

2 tbsp chopped fresh mint
several large basil sprigs, leaves shredded
225 g/8 oz feta cheese, crumbled
salt and freshly ground black pepper

■ Press all the spinach leaves into a large saucepan while still dripping wet. Put a lid on the pan and place it over high heat. Cook, shaking the pan often, for about 5 minutes, or until the spinach has wilted and shrunk. Stir the leaves, cover and cook for a further 2 minutes or so, until tender. Drain well, then replace the spinach in the pan and add the knob of butter. Cover and leave over low heat to keep hot.

■ Heat the oil, then stir-fry the spring onions, flageolet beans and courgettes for 5 minutes, until the courgettes are just cooked. Spoon the spinach on to one large or four individual serving plates. Toss the mint, basil and feta into the vegetables, and add seasoning to taste. Spoon the vegetables over the spinach and serve the dish at once.

RICE À LA PROVENÇALE

— FRANCE —

SERVES 4

600 ml/1 pt water
½ tsp salt
225 g/8 oz long-grain rice
4 tbsp oil
25 g/1 oz butter
2 onions, chopped
2 garlic cloves, crushed
salt and freshly ground black pepper
2 red peppers, seeded and blanched

4 courgettes, washed and thinly sliced
½ tsp basil
4 tbsp white wine
8 tomatoes, skinned and chopped
garnish
1 tbsp chopped capers
2 hard-boiled eggs
8 green olives, stoned
2 tbsp chopped parsley or chervil

■ Bring the water to the boil, add the salt and cook the rice, stirring to separate the grains. Cover and simmer gently until all the water has been absorbed.

■ Heat the oil and butter and cook the onions over a low heat for about 4 minutes. Add the garlic. Dice the peppers and add with the courgettes, basil and wine. Stir gently until cooked, about 5 minutes. Lastly, stir in the tomatoes. Gently fold in the cooked rice and season well. Add the chopped capers and turn into a heated serving dish.

■ Decorate with hard-boiled eggs, green olives and chopped herbs.

PEPPER **S**AUCE **P**ASTA

— ITALY —

SERVES 4–6

4 tbsp olive oil
2 garlic cloves, finely chopped
225 g/8 oz rindless bacon rashers, diced
1 onion, halved and thinly sliced
2 red peppers, seeded, quartered lengthways and cut in strips

2 green peppers, seeded, quartered lengthways and cut in strips
50 g/2 oz pine nuts
6 tbsp raisins
salt and freshly ground black pepper
150 ml/¼ pt dry sherry
450 g/1 lb tagliatelle

■ Heat the oil in a large frying pan. Add the garlic, bacon, onion and red and green peppers. Cook, stirring often, for 5 minutes. Stir in the pine kernels and raisins with plenty of seasoning, then continue to cook, stirring occasionally, for 15 minutes.

■ Pour in the sherry and bring to the boil. Boil for 3 minutes. Taste and adjust the seasoning.

■ Cook the pasta in a large pan of boiling salted water until just tender. Drain, transfer to a serving dish, cover with the sauce and serve at once

SWEET ONION PIE

UNITED STATES

Sweet onions sautéed slowly until they are golden, Swiss cheese and savoury custard: this pie is delicious! Serve it as a main dish with a green salad and French bread, or as a side dish with grilled meat or fish. Use any sweet onion.

SERVES 6

23-cm/9-in deep pastry case, pre-baked
3 medium sweet onions, about 450 g/1 lb peeled and thinly sliced
50 g/2 oz butter
125 g/4 oz Swiss cheese, grated

3 eggs, beaten with a fork
150 ml/¼ pt soured cream
5 tbsp milk
1 tsp salt
¼ tsp pepper

■ Melt the butter in a large frying pan. Add the onions and sauté over low heat until they are golden brown, 25 to 30 minutes. (If your pan isn't very large, you may have to use two frying pans.) Put the onions in the pastry case. Sprinkle the cheese over the onions. Preheat the oven to 180°C/350°F/Gas Mark 4.

■ Make the custard by combining the remaining ingredients. Pour over onions and bake until set and lightly browned around edges, about 45 minutes. Serve warm.

STUFFED COURGETTES

— INDIA —

SERVES 4

4 large courgettes
1 onion, peeled
1 red pepper, seeded
1 green pepper, seeded
4 tbsp vegetable oil
1 garlic clove, crushed
125 g/4 oz cooked long-grain rice
125 g/4 oz cooked chicken (optional)
2 tbsp cooked sweetcorn
¼ tsp cumin
½ tsp garam masala
salt and freshly ground pepper
150 ml/¼ pt sour cream
1 tbsp chopped parsley

■ Wash the courgettes and cut a thin slice lengthwise across the top of each. Scoop out the flesh and chop into small pieces. Cut a small slice off the bottom if any of the courgettes are tipping over when laid flat.

■ Prepare the vegetables by dicing the onion and peppers. Heat the oil in a frying pan and cook the onion for 3 minutes. Then add the peppers and garlic. Cook for a further 3 minutes.

■ Add the rice and stir well. If you are using chicken, dice and add at this stage. Sprinkle in the sweetcorn and the seasonings over a low heat and mix for 1 minute.

■ Brush the courgette shells with oil and fill with the rice mixture. Pour the sour cream over and bake in the oven for 20 minutes. Serve sprinkled with chopped parsley.

STIR-FRIED VEGETABLES IN A NUOC MAM SAUCE

— VIETNAM —

SERVES 4

2 carrots, finely sliced
125 g/4 oz bamboo shoots, thinly sliced
1 Chinese cabbage, stems only, diced
125 g/4 oz French beans
25 g/1 oz wood ear fungus, soaked in warm water for 15 minutes and roughly chopped
½ tsp vegetable oil
2 garlic cloves, crushed
3 slices root ginger, peeled and cut in slivers
125 g/4 oz beansprouts
salt and freshly ground black pepper
½ tbsp cornflour
1 tbsp Nuoc Mam sauce or 1 tbsp light soy sauce

■ In a large saucepan half full of water boil the carrots for 10 minutes. Add the bamboo shoots, Chinese cabbage, French beans and wood ear fungus and cook for a further 5 minutes. Drain and reserve.

■ Heat the oil in a wok and stir-fry the garlic and ginger for 2 minutes. Add the beansprouts and stir-fry for 30 seconds. Stir in all the reserved vegetables and season with salt and black pepper. Stir-fry for 2 minutes. Mix the cornflour and Nuoc Mam sauce with a little water and fold into the vegetables to bind them. Stir for 1 minute more, then serve.

AUBERGINE RICE CASSEROLE

TURKEY

SERVES 4

2 aubergines, washed
salt
juice of 1 lemon
225 g/8 oz long-grain
 rice
25 g/1 oz butter
4 tbsp vegetable oil
2 onions, peeled and
 finely chopped
2 garlic cloves, crushed
1 carrot, scraped and
 grated

425 g/15 oz canned
 peeled tomatoes
1 tsp tomato purée
4 tbsp white wine
4 tbsp stock or water
1 tsp dried basil or 2 tsp
 freshly chopped basil
 leaves
125 g/4 oz mushrooms,
 washed and sliced
4 tbsp grated cheese
 (preferably Parmesan)

■ Cut the aubergines into thick slices lengthwise. Arrange on a tray lined with kitchen paper. Sprinkle with a little salt and lemon juice. Allow to stand for 20 to 30 minutes.

■ Cook the rice in 1 ltr/1¾ pt boiling salted water for 10 minutes. It should still be firm. Drain and toss in 15 g/1 oz butter. Place in the bottom of an oiled ovenproof dish or shallow casserole.

■ Meanwhile, heat half the oil in a saucepan and cook the onion and garlic gently for about 4 minutes over a low heat. Add the grated carrot and stir for a further 1 minute.

■ Add the canned tomatoes, tomato purée, wine and stock or water with the basil. Stir until the tomatoes are broken down. Simmer gently for 30 minutes.

■ Pat the sliced aubergine dry with kitchen paper. Heat the remaining oil in a frying pan and fry the aubergine on a medium heat until golden brown. Drain on kitchen paper. Preheat the oven to 180˚C/350˚F/Gas Mark 4.

■ Layer half the aubergine over the rice and season well. Add half the tomato sauce. Top with a further layer of aubergine and a layer of sliced mushrooms. Pour over the remaining tomato sauce. Sprinkle with grated cheese. Bake in the oven for 20 to 30 minutes until the rice is tender.

POTATO GNOCCHI

ITALY

These little dumplings may be served with any sauce you like. If you are looking for a simple, satisfying supper, simply toss them with butter, freshly ground black pepper and lots of grated Parmesan.

SERVES 4

450 g/1 lb potatoes
25 g/1 oz butter
175 g/6 oz strong plain
 flour

1 tsp salt
1 egg
a little freshly grated
 nutmeg

■ Boil the potatoes in their skins until tender, about 20 to 30 minutes, depending on size. Drain and peel the potatoes under cold running water, then mash them and rub through a fine sieve into a bowl.

■ Add the butter to the potato, then stir in the flour and salt, followed by the egg and a little nutmeg. Mix the ingredients with a spoon at first, then use your hand to bring them together into a dough. Knead lightly until smooth.

■ Bring a large pan of salted water to the boil. Shape a lump of the dough into a thick sausage, then cut off small pieces, about 2.5 cm/1 in long, and indent each piece, either with your finger or with a fork. Drop the gnocchi into the boiling water, bring back to the boil and cook for 4 to 5 minutes. The water must not boil too rapidly and the cooked gnocchi should be firm and tender – do not overcook them or they will become soggy and watery. Use a slotted spoon to remove the gnocchi from the pan if you are cooking them in batches. Drain well and serve at once with melted butter, pepper and Parmesan, or the sauce of your choice.

SPAGHETTI WITH WALNUTS AND OLIVES

—— ITALY ——

SERVES 4

450 g/1 lb spaghetti
75 ml/3 fl oz olive oil
knob of butter
1 garlic clove, crushed
  (optional)
175 g/6 oz walnuts, finely
  chopped

125 g/4 oz black olives,
  roughly chopped
2 tbsp capers, chopped
4 tbsp chopped parsley
salt and freshly ground
  black pepper

■ Cook the spaghetti in a large pan of boiling salted water. Meanwhile, heat the oil and butter with the garlic (if using) until the butter melts. Stir in the walnuts, cook gently for 2 minutes, then add the olives, capers, parsley, a little salt and plenty of freshly ground black pepper. Pour the mixture over the drained spaghetti, toss well and serve at once.

ARTICHOKE HEART AND BROAD BEAN STEW

—— GREECE ——

SERVES 6–8

freshly squeezed juice of 3
  lemons
600 ml/1 pt water
8 fresh globe artichokes
3 tbsp olive oil
1 large onion, finely
  chopped
3 garlic cloves, crushed
900 g/2 lb fresh broad
  beans, podded, washed
  and drained (or
  450 g/1 lb frozen

broad beans)
125 g/4 oz fennel, thinly
  sliced
salt and freshly ground
  black pepper, to taste
½ tsp caster sugar

SAUCE
50 ml/2 fl oz olive oil
1 tbsp plain flour
freshly squeezed juice of
  1 lemon

■ Place the juice of 2 of the lemons in a large bowl with the water. To prepare the artichokes, use a pair of kitchen scissors and cut off all but 2.5 cm/1 in of the stems, then cut away the tough outer leaves. Cut off about 6 cm/2½ in from the top of each artichoke. Open out the leaves of the artichokes and, using a teaspoon, scrape out the hairy chokes and discard. Submerge the prepared artichokes in the lemon water.

■ Heat the olive oil in a large, deep frying pan and sauté the onion and garlic for 3 to 4 minutes, until the onion has softened. Add the broad beans to the pan and cook for a further 3 to 4 minutes. Add the artichokes, fennel, salt and freshly ground black pepper, sugar and the remaining lemon juice. Add enough water to the pan to almost cover, then reduce the heat, place the lid on the pan and simmer for 50 to 60 minutes, or until the vegetables are tender.

■ Using a slotted spoon, transfer the artichokes and bean mixture to a warm serving plate and tent with foil to keep warm. To make the sauce, heat 3 tablespoons of olive oil in a medium-sized saucepan and stir in the flour to make a thick paste. Cook the paste for about 1 to 2 minutes, or until it turns a light golden colour.

■ Whisk in the lemon juice and then the cooking juices from the vegetables into the saucepan. Cook over gentle heat, stirring continuously, until the sauce has thickened and there are no lumps. Season with salt and freshly ground black pepper. Remove the foil tent from the vegetables and pour the sauce over them.

CAULIFLOWER AND CELERY STIR-FRY

─── UNITED KINGDOM ───

SERVES 4–6

3 tbsp oil
1 small onion, halved and
   thinly sliced
½ small cauliflower, broken
   into small florets
1 celery heart, thinly sliced
salt and freshly ground
   black pepper

50 g/2 oz stoned black
   olives, sliced
1 sweet eating apple,
   cored and roughly
   chopped
1 tbsp capers, chopped
1 tbsp demerara sugar
1–2 tbsp cider vinegar

■ Heat the oil and stir-fry the onion for 5 minutes before adding the cauliflower and celery. Stir-fry the vegetables until they are lightly cooked – they should not taste raw but should still be crunchy. This takes about 15 minutes, depending on the heat and size of the pan.

■ Add the seasoning, olives, apple and capers, and continue to stir-fry for 2 minutes. Make a well in the middle of the vegetables and add the sugar and 1 tablespoon of the vinegar. Stir the juices until the sugar dissolves, then toss the small amount of dressing with the vegetables. Taste and add the remaining vinegar if liked. Serve at once.

BLUE **C**HEESE **R**ICE **Q**UICHE

FRANCE

SERVES 4

50 g/2 oz cooked long-
   grain rice
75 g/3 oz blue cheese,
   crumbled
2 eggs
2 tbsp single cream
salt and freshly ground
   pepper
pinch of cayenne pepper
¼ tsp dry mustard

2 tsp chopped parsley

SHORTCRUST PASTRY
125 g/4 oz plain flour
pinch of salt
25 g/1 oz butter or
   margarine
25 g/1 oz white fat
1½ tbsp cold water

■ Make up the pastry by sieving the flour and salt into a bowl. Add the fat in small lumps and rub in with the fingertips until the mixture resembles fine breadcrumbs. Add the water, a few drops at a time, and mix to a firm dough. Rest in the refrigerator for 15 minutes.

■ Preheat the oven to 200°C/400°F/Gas Mark 6. Roll the pastry out in a neat circle to fit a 17.5-cm/7-in flan ring. Lift the pastry on to the rolling pin and over the ring, then ease it in to avoid stretching. Trim the top with the rolling pin. Line with greaseproof paper and some baking beans, then bake for 15 minutes. Remove the paper and baking beans and cook for a further 5 minutes. Remove and allow to cool slightly. Lower the temperature to 180°C/350°F/Gas Mark 4.

■ Mix the crumbled blue cheese with the rice and arrange in the bottom of the pastry case. Beat the eggs in a cup, and add the cream and seasonings. Pour over the rice and cheese. Sprinkle with chopped parsley. Bake for 20 minutes at the lower temperature until set and golden.

POTATO AND **T**OMATO **P**IE

PORTUGAL

Two of Portugal's favourite vegetables are brought together in this simple yet tasty recipe from the Douro. It is a useful way of using leftover cooked potatoes.

SERVES 4

about 6 boiled or steamed
   medium-sized potatoes,
   thinly sliced
red pepper paste (see
   page 87), for spreading
1 bunch parsley
1 garlic clove
1 fresh red chilli, seeded

3 tbsp virgin olive oil, plus
   extra for trickling
squeeze of lemon juice
salt and pepper
575 g/1¼ lb well-
   flavoured tomatoes,
   skinned, seeded and
   sliced

■ Preheat the oven to 200°C/400°F/Gas Mark 6.
■ Lay the potato slices in a well-oiled, shallow baking dish. Spread thinly with red pepper paste.
■ Chop the parsley, garlic and chilli and mix together with the oil. Add lemon juice and seasoning to taste, then spread half over the potatoes. Cover with the tomatoes and spoon over the remaining parsley mixture. Trickle over a little oil and bake for 30 to 40 minutes. Serve warm, not straight from the oven.

SAVOURY RICE RING WITH VEGETABLE CURRY

INDIA

SERVES 4

225 g/8 oz basmati or
  long-grain rice
3 tbsp oil
1 onion, peeled and finely
  chopped
¼ green pepper, washed,
  seeded and diced
1 red pepper, washed,
  seeded and diced
salt and freshly ground
  black pepper
¼ tsp garam masala

VEGETABLE CURRY
1 large onion, peeled
1 garlic clove, crushed
2.5 cm/1 in fresh root
  ginger
1 level tbsp mild curry
  powder
200 g/7 oz canned
  chopped tomatoes
1 carrot, scraped
1 potato, peeled
1 small cauliflower
2 tbsp oil
1 tsp ground cumin
1 tbsp lemon juice
1 bay leaf

■ Rinse the rice well. Partly cook for about 10 minutes after it has come to the boil. Rinse off excess liquid with cold water. Drain well.

■ Place 2 tablespoons oil in a frying pan and cook the onion over a low heat for 3 minutes. Add half the green and red pepper and continue cooking for a further 3 minutes. Tip the rice into the pan with the vegetables. Mix well with seasoning and garam masala. Preheat the oven to 180°C/350°F/Gas Mark 4.

■ Oil a ring mould. Mix the remaining oil with the rice mixture and place it in the mould. Cook in the oven for 15 minutes.

■ Meanwhile, chop half the onion into thin rings and set aside. Chop the remaining half and blend it with the garlic, root ginger and curry powder, mixed with 2 tablespoons tomato juice.

■ Cut the carrot into rings and dice the potato. Boil in a little salted water for 5 minutes. Drain and retain the vegetable water.

■ Cut the cauliflower into florets and steep in cold water. Heat the oil and fry the onion rings for 3 minutes. Remove to another saucepan.

■ Fry the curry paste on a fairly high heat until brown. Add to the onion saucepan with the remaining juice of the tomatoes and 300 ml/½ pt vegetable water.

■ Add the carrots, potato, remaining red and green peppers, cauliflower florets, ground cumin, lemon juice, salt, bay leaf and chopped tomatoes. Bring to the boil and simmer for 25 minutes, stirring well to mix the ingredients and to avoid sticking. Add the mushrooms and allow to simmer for a further 5 minutes. Remove the bay leaf and taste for seasoning.

■ After removing the rice from the oven, leave for a few minutes to shrink. Gently turn the rice out of the mould on to a heated serving plate. Pour the vegetable curry into the centre of the ring. Turn excess curry on to a separate dish and serve with other suitable curry accompaniments, such as poppadoms and mango chutney.

LENTILS WITH MUSHROOMS AND ALMONDS

—— UNITED KINGDOM ——

*A delicious vegetarian main course, this is an ideal mid-week feast as
a change from meat-based main dishes.*

SERVES 4

225 g/8 oz green lentils,
   cooked
450 g/1 lb button
   mushrooms, sliced
1 tsp ground mace
salt and pepper
4 tbsp olive oil

75 g/3 oz blanched
   almonds, split in half
knob of butter
225 g/8 oz oyster
   mushrooms
4 tbsp snipped chives

■ The lentils should be freshly cooked, drained and
set aside in a covered pan so that they stay hot while
the rest of the dish is prepared.

■ Mix the button mushrooms with the mace and
plenty of seasoning. Heat the oil and stir-fry the
mushrooms briskly until they begin to brown. When
they give up their juices, continue stir-frying until all the
liquid has evaporated and the mushrooms are greatly

reduced in volume. At this stage they have a good,
concentrated flavour; they should be dark in colour
and most of the liquid in the pan should be the oil in
which they have cooked.

■ Use a slotted spoon to remove the mushrooms from
the pan and add them to the lentils. Cover and set
aside. Stir-fry the almonds in the oil remaining in the
pan until they are golden, then add them to the lentils.
Fork the almonds and mushrooms into the lentils, then
transfer the mixture to a serving dish or individual
bowls.

■ Melt the butter in the pan and stir-fry the oyster
mushrooms over fairly high heat for a minute or so –
they should be very lightly cooked. If the mushrooms
are overcooked they will collapse. Stir in the chives
with a little seasoning, and spoon the mixture over the
lentils, scraping any juices from the cooking pan. Serve
at once.

TAGLIATELLE WITH CHICK-PEAS AND BASIL

ITALY

SERVES 4

450 g/1 lb tagliatelle
  verdi
4 tbsp olive oil
1 garlic clove, crushed
6 tbsp snipped chives
4 sage leaves, chopped

salt and freshly ground
  black pepper
2 x 400-g/14-oz cans
  chick-peas, drained
6 basil sprigs

■ Cook the pasta in a large pan of boiling salted water until just tender. Meanwhile, heat the olive oil, garlic, chives, sage, salt and freshly ground black pepper with the chick-peas in a large saucepan for about 3 minutes. The idea is to heat the ingredients rather than to cook them. Add the drained pasta and toss well. Leave the pan over the lowest heat setting while you use scissors to snip the basil sprigs over the pasta, discarding any tough stalks. Mix lightly and serve.

MEATLESS STUFFED VEGETABLES

GREECE

This recipe originates from the island of Crete, where the use of rice as the main ingredient for stuffings is most common. The addition of raisins, pine nuts or almonds makes this a truly Cretan creation.

SERVES 8–10

8–10 firm, ripe vegetables,
  including tomatoes,
  peppers, courgettes and
  aubergines
75 ml/3 fl oz olive oil
6 spring onions, finely
  chopped
225 g/8 oz long-grain
  rice
2 garlic cloves, crushed

1 tsp ground cinnamon
75 g/3 oz seedless raisins
75 g/3 oz toasted pine
  nuts
salt and freshly ground
  black pepper, to taste
4 tbsp chopped fresh
  parsley
3 tbsp chopped fresh mint

■ To prepare the vegetables, slice the tops off the tomatoes, peppers, courgettes and aubergines. Scoop out the seeds and flesh from the tomatoes and place in a bowl. Do the same with the aubergines and courgettes, remembering to discard the bitter seeds from the aubergines. Scoop out the seeds from the peppers and discard. Keep each vegetable top intact.
■ In a large frying pan, heat 2 tablespoons of the olive oil and add the onions. Cook for 3 minutes, then stir in the rice, garlic, cinnamon, raisins, pine nuts and the seeds and pulp reserved from the vegetables. Add enough water to cover the rice and simmer, covered, for 7 to 10 minutes, or until the rice is tender and most of the liquid has been absorbed.
■ Stir the seasoning and herbs into the rice filling and remove from the heat. Preheat the oven to 180°C/350°F/Gas Mark 4. Stuff the vegetables with the rice filling and place the tops on each vegetable. Arrange the vegetables in a large roasting pan and pour in enough water to just cover the base of the pan.
■ Drizzle over the remaining olive oil and bake for 50 to 60 minutes, or until the vegetables are tender. Baste several times during cooking, but try not to rearrange the vegetables as they may break apart. They can be served warm, but are just as delicious served cold.

PASTA WITH SUN-DRIED TOMATO SALSA

— MEXICO —

The intense flavours of this powerful salsa may clash in concentrated form. When it is tossed with pasta, however, the flavours meld and become complementary.

SERVES 2

3 tbsp olive oil

6 garlic cloves, crushed

1 tsp crushed dried chillies

1 red pepper, cored, seeded and cut into quarters

125 g/4 oz sun-dried tomatoes, packed in oil

1 tbsp chopped fresh basil

4 rashers bacon, cooked and crumbled

50 g/2 oz sliced black olives

340–450 g/12 oz–1 lb pasta

grated Parmesan cheese

■ Heat the oil in a small frying pan over low heat. Add the garlic and the dried chillies. Cook slowly, stirring often and pressing the garlic to release the juices, until the garlic is lightly browned, 5 to 8 minutes. The heat must be very low or the garlic may scorch and turn bitter. Remove from the heat and let soak while you prepare the other ingredients.

■ Cook the red pepper skin side down over a barbecue fire, or skin side up under a grill, until the skin is blackened. Remove from the heat and place it in a plastic bag to steam for 10 minutes. Peel off the skin and chop the red pepper.

■ Chop the sun-dried tomatoes and put them into a small bowl with the basil. Add the bacon, garlic mixture, red pepper and sliced olives. Cook the pasta in plenty of boiling salted water until just tender. Drain well, and then toss with the salsa and Parmesan cheese.

INDEX

almonds
  almond-stuffed pork with sherry and cream 86
  chicken with pounded almond sauce 30
  lentils with mushrooms and 187
  muscat baked almond chicken 28
anchovies, steak with olives and 50
apples
  lamb pilaf 121
  pork loin with apple preserves 76
  roast goose with fruity stuffing 42
  spinach with walnuts and 172
artichoke heart and broad bean stew 182
asparagus supreme 166
aubergines
  aubergine rice casserole 180
  in coconut sauce 175
  green beef curry 67
  mushroom-stuffed 170
  red chicken curry 19
  sautéed lamb with 125

bacon
  cabbage with kabanos 98
  and pasta hotpot 114
  pasta with sun-dried tomato salsa 189
  pepper sauce pasta 177
  pork with beans 80
  simmered beef with turnips and carrots 64
bamboo shoots 9
  pork chow mein 86
  Szechuan noodles 88
barbecued Isla Bonita pork 76
barbecue sauce, pork spare ribs in 89
bass
  spicy seafood salad 163
  steamed fish curry 150
  Yucatan style 157
beansprouts 9
  chicken salad with grapefruit, mint and lemon grass 22
  lamb, beansprout and bean salad 110
beef
  carne con chile Colorado 53
  cholent 58
  in coconut milk 68
  enchiladas with red chilli sauce 54
  Greek hamburgers 59
  green curry 67
  hamburgers with spicy tomato sauce 63
  herring, meat and beetroot salad 129
  with lemon grass and mushrooms 66
  Madras beef curry 64
  meatballs with fresh tomato sauce 52
  Mexican beef tzimmes 62

minced, plantain rings with 55
  and onion stew 68
  in oyster sauce 56
  and pasta hotpot 114
  picadillo 66
  rolls, stuffed 69
  ropas viejas 60
  salt, and lamb stew 105
  simmered, with turnips and carrots 64
  steak with anchovies and olives 50
  steak tartare 60
  stew, spicy 50
  stroganoff 56
beetroot salad, herring, meat and 129
Biscay Bay sole with cream and shellfish 154
black beans
  black bean salsa, lamb with 118
  feijoada 73
brandy cream sauce, pork fillets in 78
bream, Yucatan style 157
broad bean and artichoke heart stew 182
buckwheat 13
  roast chicken with 33
butter beans, pork with 80

cabbage with kabanos 98
calypso chicken 35
calypso cod steaks 135
capers, pork chops with peppers and 84
carbonara, pasta 82
Caribbean coconut chicken 27
carne con chile Colorado 53
carp 13
  sweet-and-sour fish 136
carrots
  carrot and potato hotpot 175
  simmered beef with turnips and 64
  spaghetti with smoked sausage and 92
cauliflower
  baked with tomatoes and feta 167

and celery stir-fry 183
celery
  and cauliflower stir-fry 183
  stir-fried pork and 72
cheese
  blue cheese rice quiche 185
  cauliflower baked with tomatoes and feta 167
  chicken in blue 21
  chicken with feta and green olives 34
  chicken and ham lasagne 37
  chicken and rice stew 41
  chunks of lamb in filo pastry 104
  lamb chops with 112
  sweet onion pie 178
chicken
  andouille and prawn jambalaya 20
  baked with potatoes and garlic 40
  in blue 21
  brochettes with orange sauce 26
  calypso 35
  Caribbean coconut 27
  casserole, Easter 24
  and chick-pea stew 32
  cilantro 16
  citrus-fried 25
  cochin-style chilli 31
  compote, sautéed 30
  curry, red 19
  with feta and green olives 34
  green curry 67
  and ham lasagne 37
  honey-rum, with mushroom sauce 17
  lemon 18
  meat and tomato stew 113
  muscat baked almond 28
  mustard-baked 28
  nasi goreng 72
  pilaf 39

poached, with melon 20
  pot pie, with cornmeal crust 40
  with pounded almond sauce 30
  and rice stew 41
  roast, with buckwheat 33
  salad with grapefruit, mint and lemon grass 22
  salsa 24
  stuffed 16
  stuffed courgettes 179
  sweet and sour 27
  with walnuts and pomegranates 19
  won tons, with vegetables 38
chick-peas
  chicken and chick-pea stew 32
  lamb knuckle stew 108
chillies
  beef enchiladas with red chilli sauce 54
  carne con chile Colorado 53
  chilli sauce 11
  cochin-style chilli chicken 31
  fettucine with prawns and chilli-cream sauce 132
  flat fish with hazelnut and chilli sauce 141
  salsa chicken 24
chorizo 12
  chorizo-rice stuffing, roast pork with 94
  tolosa red bean stew with pork 100
chow mein
  pork 86
  tofu 169
citrus-fried chicken 25
clams
  mixed fish and shellfish stew 138
  pork with 85
  Tyrean 158
cochin-style chilli chicken 31
coconut
  beef in coconut milk 68
  Caribbean coconut chicken 27
  red chicken curry 19
  sauce, aubergines in 175
cod
  ackee and salt fish 162
  curried fish fillets 161
  fish in horseradish sauce 149
  fish and vegetable casserole 158
  with saffron 144
  salt, with onions and potatoes 152
  steaks, calypso 135
cornmeal crust, chicken pot pie with 40
courgettes
  crab and courgette salad 141
  crab-stuffed 133
  pork with 80
  stuffed 179
crab
  and courgette salad 141
  crab-stuffed courgettes 133
  crab-stuffed fish 143
  stir-fried seafood with mint,

garlic and chillies 136
Creole-style marinated fish 140
cumin, pork casserole with 98
curry
  fish fillets 161
  gingery pork chops with
    curried mango 101
  green beef 67
  lamb with lentils 110
  Madras beef 64
  northern pork 97
  pork chops with rice pilaf 97
  red chicken 19
  steamed fish 150
  vegetable, savoury rice ring
    with 186

dill
  and ginger vinaigrette, poached
    salmon fillets with 160
  pasta with salmon, mustard and
    128
  roast chicken with buckwheat
    33
drunken squid 133
duck
  with ginger sauce 44
  green curry 67

Easter chicken casserole 24
egg noodles 13
  pork chow mein 86
  Szechuan noodles 88
  tofu chow mein 169
eggs
  chicken salad with grapefruit,
    mint and lemon grass 22
  nasi goreng 72
  rice a la Provençale 176
feijoada 73
feta
  cauliflower baked with
    tomatoes and 167
  chicken with green olives and
    34
  chunks of lamb in filo pastry
    104
filo 13
  chunks of lamb in 104
flageolet beans with spinach 176
flounder
  pecan-encrusted 143
  steamed fish curry 150
French beans
  lamb, beansprout and bean
    salad 110
  and new potatoes in pesto 171

garlic
  chicken baked with potatoes
    and 40
  lamb in a hot garlic sauce 112
  prawns fried with pepper and
    153
  red mullet with 128
ginger
  gingery pork chops with
    curried mango 101
  oriental ginger lamb 116
  sauce, duck with 44
glass noodles 13
  casseroled prawns with 156
gnocchi 180
goat
  curried, with lentils 110
  and salt beef stew 105
  stewed, Sint Maarten 119
goose, roast, with fruity stuffing
  42
grapefruit, mint and lemon grass,

chicken salad with 22
grilled spicy-marmalade turkey
  cutlets 43
gumbo, seafood, with okra 154

haddock, fish and vegetable
  casserole 158
halibut
  curried fish fillets 161
  with saffron 144
ham
  chicken and ham lasagne 37
  chicken pot pie with cornmeal
    crust 40
  meat and mushroom patties in
    sauce 92
  nasi goreng 72
  pasta carbonara 82
hamburgers
  Greek 59
  with spicy tomato sauce 63
hazelnut and chilli sauce, flat fish
  with 141
Ho Chi Minh duck 44
hominy 13
  and pork stew 82
honey-rum chicken with
  mushroom sauce 17
horseradish sauce, fish in 149

jambalaya, prawn, chicken
  andouille and 20

kabanos 12
  cabbage with 98
kebabs
  lamb 123
  mince 120
  spicy shark 148
  sweet potato and okra 170
kidney beans
  cholent 58
  lamb with black bean salsa 118
  Mexican beef tzimmes 62
  red beans and rice 169
  tolosa red bean stew with pork
    100

lamb
  pilaf 121
  baked papaya with meat filling
    124
  with black bean salsa 118
  braised 123
  chops, spiced 100
  chops with cheese 112
  chunks, in filo pastry 104
  curried, with lentils 110
  fried, with lemon juice 108
  fried, with paprika and vinegar 115
  in a hot garlic sauce 112
  kebabs 123
  knuckle stew 108
  meatballs in tomato sauce 107
  meat and tomato stew 113
  mince kebabs 120
  minted, with vegetables 122
  oriental ginger 116
  and pasta hotpot 114
  salad, lamb, beansprout and bean
    110
  and salt beef stew 105
  sautéed, with aubergine 125
  spicy, with peppers 116
  spicy mince with peas 104
  stew, spicy, with mint and sage 111
  stewed, Sint Maarten 119
  stuffed chicken 16
  stuffed peppers 106
  tikka 115

lasagne, chicken and ham 37
leeks
  lemon-scented pompano on
    spinach and 145
  pumpkin with 174
lemon chicken 18
lemon grass 9
  beef with mushrooms and 66
  chicken salad with grapefruit, mint
    and 22
lemon juice, fried lamb with 108
lemon sauce, meat and rice balls in
  95
lemon-scented pompano on spinach
  and leeks 145
lentils
  curried lamb with 110
  with mushrooms and almonds 187
liver with mint 48

Madras beef curry 64
mangoes
  gingery pork chops with curried
    101
  Mexican beef tzimmes 62
  poached chicken with melon 20
marmalade, grilled spicy-marmalade
  turkey cutlets 43
meatloaf 49
melon, poached chicken with 20
mint
  liver with 48
  minted lamb with vegetables 122
  spicy lamb stew with sage and 111
monkfish
  fish and vegetable casserole 158
  with saffron 144
  seafood medley 153
mullet
  crab-stuffed fish 143
  Creole-style marinated fish 140
  red, with garlic 128
muscat baked almond chicken 28
mushrooms
  beef with lemon grass and 66
  beef stroganoff 56
  calypso chicken 35
  chicken and ham lasagne 37
  chicken pot pie with cornmeal
    crust 40
  Easter chicken casserole 24
  honey-rum chicken with
    mushroom sauce 17
  lentils with almonds and 187
  mushroom-stuffed aubergines 170
  turkey escalopes with white wine
    and mushroom sauce 42
mussels
  Biscay Bay sole with cream and
    shellfish 154
  mixed fish and shellfish stew 138
  mussel pancakes 135
  seafood lasagne 138
  seafood medley 153
  stir-fried seafood with mint, garlic
    and chillies 136
  Tyrean 158
mustard-baked chicken 28

nasi goreng 72

okra
  seafood gumbo with 154
  sweet potato and okra kebabs 170
olives
  green, chicken with feta and 34
  spaghetti with walnuts and 182
  steak with anchovies and 50
onion pie, sweet 178
onion stew, beef and 68

orange sauce, chicken brochettes
  with 26
oriental ginger lamb 116
oyster sauce 12
  beef in 56

pancakes, mussel 135
papaya
  baked, with meat filling 124
  sautéed chicken compote 30
paprika
  fried lamb with vinegar and 115
  sauce, skate with peas and
    potatoes in 146
pasta
  agnolotti 74
  asparagus supreme 166
  carbonara 82
  fettucine with prawns and chilli-
    cream sauce 132
  and lamb hotpot 114
  pepper sauce 177
  pork and rosemary ravioli 74
  with salmon, dill and mustard 128
  seafood lasagne 138
  smoked tofu with 168
  spaghetti with smoked sausage and
    carrots 92
  spaghetti with walnuts and olives
    182
  with sun-dried tomato salsa 189
patties, meat and mushroom, in
  sauce 92
peas
  skate with potatoes and, in paprika
    sauce 146
  spicy mince with 104
pecan-encrusted flounder 143
peppers
  chicken and chick-pea stew 32
  pepper sauce pasta 177
  pork chops with capers and 84
  pork with clams 85
  sausage and pepper stew 87
  spicy lamb with 116
  stuffed 106
perch, spicy seafood salad 163
Pernod, pork with 75
pesto, French beans and new
  potatoes in 171
picadillo 66
pike, sweet-and-sour fish 136
plaice, crab-stuffed fish 143
plantains 8, 55
  plantain rings with minced beef 55
poached chicken with melon 20
pomegranates, chicken with walnuts
  and 19
pompano 13
  lemon-scented, on spinach and
    leeks 145
pork 129
  almond-stuffed, with sherry and
    cream 86
  balls, sweet-sour 78
  with beans 80
  cabbage with kabanos 98
  carne con chile Colorado 53
  casserole with cumin 98
  chicken salad with grapefruit, mint
    and lemon grass 22
  chops, curried, with rice pilaf 97
  chops, gingery, with curried mango
    101
  chops with capers and peppers 84
  chow mein 86
  with clams 85
  with courgettes 80
  feijoada 73
  fillets in brandy cream sauce 78

green curry 67
and hominy stew 82
Isla Bonita, barbecued 76
loin with apple preserves 76
meat and mushroom patties in
    sauce 92
meat and rice balls in lemon sauce
    95
northern pork curry 97
and pasta hotpot 114
with Pernod 75
Puerto Rican-style roast 91
roast, calypso 99
roast, with chorizo-rice stuffing 94
roast, with rhubarb sauce 93
and rosemary ravioli 74
satay-flavour 81
spare ribs in barbecue sauce 89
steamed minced, with saltfish 100
stir-fried, and celery 72
Szechuan noodles 88
tolosa red bean stew with 100
and wheat 79
potatoes
    carrot and potato hotpot 175
    chicken baked with garlic and 40
    cholent 58
    French beans and new potatoes in
        pesto 171
    gnocchi 180
    potato and tomato pie 185
    salt cod with onions and 152
    skate with peas and, in paprika
        sauce 146
prawns
    casseroled, with glass noodles 156
    chicken andouille and prawn
        jambalaya 20
    chicken salad with grapefruit, mint
        and lemon grass 22
    Creole 130
    fettucine with, and chilli-cream
        sauce 132
    fried with garlic and pepper 153
    mixed fish and shellfish stew 138
    nasi goreng 72
    seafood lasagne 138
    seafood medley 153
    spicy seafood salad 163
    stir-fried seafood with mint, garlic
        and chillies 136
pumpkin with leeks 174

quiche, blue cheese rice 185

red chicken curry 19
rhubarb sauce, roast pork with 93
rice
    a la Provençale 176
    aubergine rice casserole 180
    blue cheese rice quiche 185
    chicken brochettes with orange
        sauce 26
    chicken pilaf 39
    chicken and rice stew 41
    curried pork chops with rice pilaf
        97
    lamb pilaf 121
    meatballs in tomato sauce 107
    meat and rice balls in lemon sauce
        95
    nasi goreng 72
    prawn Creole 130
    red beans and 169
    ring, savoury, with vegetable curry
        186
    roast pork with chorizo-rice stuffing
        94
    seafood gumbo with okra 154
    stuffed beef rolls 69

stuffed courgettes 179
stuffed peppers 106
roast chicken with buckwheat 33
roast goose with fruity stuffing 42
ropas viejas 60
rosemary and pork ravioli 74
rub-a-dub fish fry 149

sage, spicy lamb stew with mint and
    111
salads
    chicken salad with grapefruit, mint
        and lemon grass 22
    crab and courgette 141
    herring, meat and beetroot 129
    lamb, beansprout and bean 110
    spicy seafood 163
salmon
    fillets poached with dill-and-ginger
        vinaigrette 160
    lake fish in mustard sauce 137
    pasta with salmon, dill and
        mustard 128
    steaks, calypso 135
    sweet-and-sour fish 136
salsa
    feijoada 73
    fettucine with prawns and chilli-
        cream sauce 132
    lamb with black bean 118
    sun-dried tomato, pasta with 189
salsa chicken 24
saltfish, steamed minced pork with
    100
satay-flavour pork 81
sausage and pepper stew 87

sautéed chicken compote 30
scallops
    lemon-scented, on spinach and
        leeks 145
    seafood medley 153
    stir-fried seafood with mint, garlic
        and chillies 136
seafood
    Biscay Bay sole with cream and
        shellfish 154
    gumbo with okra 154
    lasagne 138
    medley 153
    mixed fish and shellfish stew 138
    salad, spicy 163
    stir-fried, with mint, garlic and
        chillies 136
    shark, kebabs, spicy 148
    simmered beef with turnips and
        carrots 64
    skate with peas and potatoes in
        paprika sauce 146
    smoked sausage, spaghetti with
        carrots and 92
snapper
    crab-stuffed fish 143
    Creole-style marinated fish 140
    red, with green sauce 130
    red, Yucatan style 157
sole
    Biscay Bay, with cream and
        shellfish 154
    crab-stuffed fish 143
    flat fish with hazelnut and chilli
        sauce 141
    steamed fish curry 150

Yucatan style 157
soufflé, sweet potato and walnut 172
spicy beef stew 50
spicy lamb with peppers 116
spicy mince with peas 104
spicy shark kebabs 148
spinach
    with apples and walnuts 172
    flageolet beans with 176
    lemon-scented pompano on leeks
        and 145
squid
    drunken 133
    Provençal 146
    seafood medley 153
    spicy seafood salad 163
    stir-fried seafood with mint, garlic
        and chillies 136
steak tartare 60
steamed fish curry 150
stir-fried pork and celery 72
stir-fried seafood with mint, garlic and
    chillies 136
stir-fried vegetables in a Nuoc Mam
    sauce 179
stir-fry, cauliflower and celery 183
sweet-and-sour fish 136
sweet onion pie 178
sweet potatoes 9
    Mexican beef tzimmes 62
    sweet potato and okra kebabs 170
    sweet potato and walnut soufflé
        172
sweet and sour chicken 27
sweet-sour pork balls 78
swordfish with saffron 144
Szechuan noodles 88

tofu 9
    chow mein 169
    smoked, with pasta 168
tolosa red bean stew with pork 100
tomatoes
    cauliflower baked with feta and
        167
    chicken and chick-pea stew 32
    chicken salsa 24
    hamburgers with spicy tomato
        sauce 63
    meatballs with fresh tomato sauce
        52
    meatballs in tomato sauce 107
    meat and tomato stew 113
    pasta with sun-dried tomato salsa
        189
    potato and tomato pie 185
    sausage and pepper stew 87
trout
    crab-stuffed fish 143
    sweet-and-sour fish 136
    Yerevan-style 150
turnips, simmered beef with carrots
    and 64
Tyrean clams or mussels 158

veal
    meatloaf 49
    meat and mushroom patties in
        sauce 92

walnuts
    chicken with pomegranates and 19
    spaghetti with olives and 182
    spinach with apples and 172
    sweet potato and walnut soufflé
        172
wheat, pork and 79
won tons, chicken, with vegetables 38

Yerevan-style trout 150